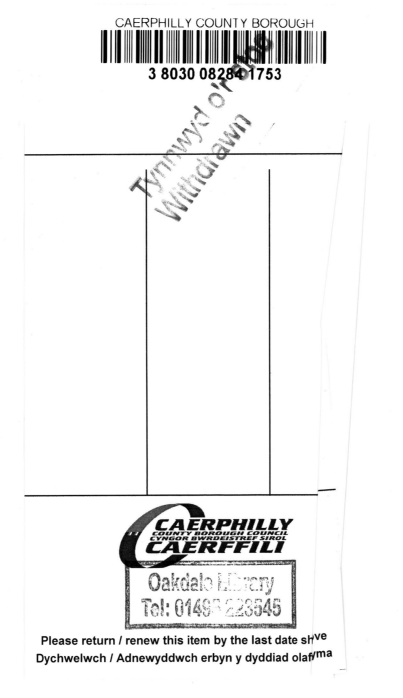

JOHNNY KINGDOM'S
WILD EXMOOR

JOHNNY KINGDOM'S

WILD EXMOOR

DAVID PARKER

With reflections on Exmoor from Johnny Kingdom

HALSGROVE

First published in Great Britain in 2015

Copyright © David Parker 2015
Unless otherwise indicated in the text all photographs in the book are taken by the author
Cover Photograph: Rupert Smith and Wendy McLean
Title page photograph: The River Exe – summer

British Library Cataloguing-in-Publication Data
A CIP record for this title is available from the British Library

ISBN 978 0 85704 262 0

HALSGROVE
Halsgrove House, Ryelands Business Park,
Bagley Road, Wellington, Somerset TA21 9PZ
Tel: 01823 653777   Fax: 01823 216796
email: sales@halsgrove.com

Part of the Halsgrove group of companies.
Information on all Halsgrove titles is
available at: www.halsgrove.com

Printed in China by the Everbest Printing Co Ltd

Contents

Reflections on Exmoor *from Johnny Kingdom*   7

Introduction   9

1. Mr Kingdom I Presume   13

PART 1 – WINTER   19

2. Big Plans and Grand Designs –
   Johnny's Winter   20

3. The Jewel in Exmoor's Crown – Red Deer   25

4. The Moor in Winter   37

PART 2 – SPRING   51

5. Birth, Marriages and (Near) Deaths –
   Johnny's Spring   52

6. Animals   58

7. The Moor in Spring   66

PART 3 – SUMMER   75

8. Fêtes Accomplished –
   Johnny's Summer   76

9. Birds of Summer   80

10. Rivers   88

11. The Moor in Summer   103

PART 4 – AUTUMN   111

12. It's the Taking Part that Counts –
    Johnny's Autumn   112

13. The Other Jewel in Exmoor's Crown –
    Exmoor Ponies   118

14. Sheep   125

15. Autumn on the Moor   134

Postscript   144

For my father
Who encouraged me

Reflections on Exmoor
from Johnny Kingdom

'WHENEVER I'VE BEEN away and I'm driving back down the North Devon Link road, I always think to myself, I'm home. Exmoor: I just love it, and I wouldn't change it for the world.'

Those are the words of Johnny Kingdom, gravedigger turned wildlife film-maker, who has lived on the moor all his life.

The idea for this book arose when my TV production company was commissioned to make a new series for ITV about Exmoor with Johnny. Since there were to be four programmes in the series, he and the director, Wendy McLean, decided to structure it around the four seasons.

As Johnny talked to us later about his seasonal round of filming, his passion for the place he calls home blazed through.

'Winter on Exmoor is hard. It's when everything starts to shut down. We went up onto Winsford Hill looking for animals to film. It had snowed heavily the night before and was bitter cold, but we found a lovely herd of ponies sheltering with their backsides to the wind. They have to put up with the weather, so think yourself lucky to be at home sitting beside the fire.

'Winter is also when I drop down to the Taw Estuary to film some of the birds that are here over the cold months: little egrets, and the curlew. There used to be loads of them on Exmoor but they've almost all gone now. I love filming summat like that, summat different from the animals on the moor.

'Then in spring, I saw dancing snakes – that's what they call it when adders fight. I've never been so close to that in my life, and we came back with brilliant shots. In the summer I filmed a nest of four barn owl chicks. Exmoor can always surprise you, and that was another sight I've never seen before, six of them in the family including the parents! We lost so many last winter when the weather was bad, but here they are, coming back.

'In the autumn, on my mate Colin's farm I found a lovely stag, a huge beast with three points on each antler. He looked so proud as he lay there with all his ladies. Another day I was out looking for a big male and I found one who was very old, but he still had a load of hinds and a lot of fight left in him. That day I filmed some of my best shots ever of fighting, roaring and mating.

Part of Exmoor's wonderful coastline

'Over the last twelve months, I've experienced things I never experienced before. Like building an underground badger house with my mate Bob Sampson. When I think of all the times I've tried it before and failed, it was a big challenge but we done it.'

For all of us it had been a brilliant year and, as Johnny reflected in June, when he was filming tiny, week-old red deer calves:

'What do you want prettier than that, my friends?'

Johnny and Julie
WENDY McLEAN

Introduction

THOUGH LIFE MIGHT seem like a series of happy (or sometimes unhappy) coincidences, it's only when you stand back and reflect on what has gone before that you come to understand just how connected events are. When I look back at my association with the wonderful landscape of Exmoor a distinct pattern of linked moments emerges, leading from my first sight of the moor in the mid-1980s to the writing of this book, thirty years later.

Most of my working life has been spent producing and directing documentary programmes for television. In 1985, I was producing a documentary for Channel 4 called *Lands at the Margin*, a film about the plight of farming communities in the uplands of south-western England. The story would focus on pastoral, hill-farming environments, including Exmoor. Travelling around the moor, doing research for the film, I soon came to enjoy the varied and contrasting landscapes cradled in a surprisingly compact area. I found I could travel across heather moorland, through deep wooded river valleys, over scintillating cliffs and along dramatic coastlines in the space of just a few miles.

Exmoor hooked me very quickly. I found myself returning to make a film that told the story of traditional Exmoor folk song, then a television walks series illustrated the ways in which the landscape had been forged over centuries by people trying to make a living from it. During the making of that series, *Secrets of the Moor*, I came across two quintessential elements of Exmoor that shaped the next twenty years of my life. One was red deer; the other Johnny Kingdom. Wanting to make a film about the first led me directly to the second and I have been making films about Exmoor with Johnny ever since. In the two decades we have been working together, he has taken me to places I could only dream of, shown me wildlife I thought I would never see and enriched my understanding of the moor in ways I could never have predicted. And he has told me stories I'm still not sure I believe.

This book is the product of those experiences and will, I hope, inspire others to enjoy and respect this extraordinary landscape.

It is structured loosely around the television series of the same name, following the cycle of winter, spring, summer and autumn on the moor, and stepping occasionally beyond the seasonal round to look more closely at some of the animals who inhabit the landscape. It highlights particular places, wildlife and people on the moor that mean something to Johnny.

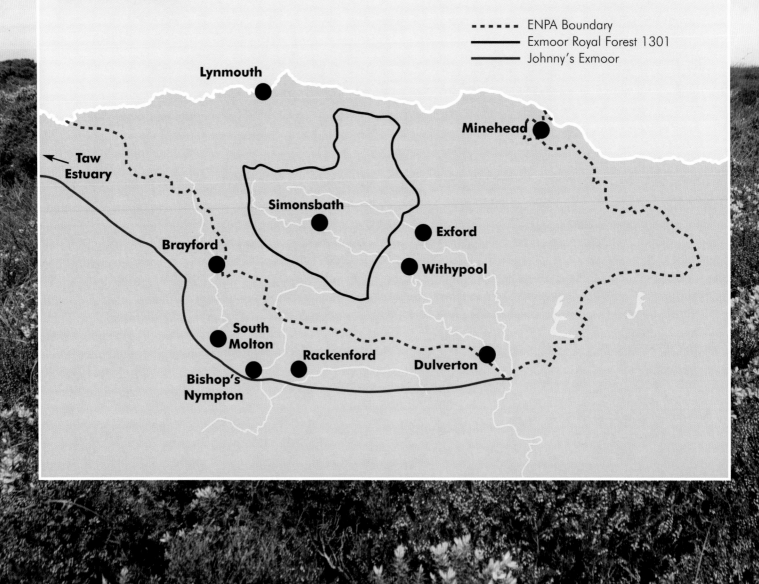

MAP OF THE AREA

- - - - - ENPA Boundary
───── Exmoor Royal Forest 1301
───── Johnny's Exmoor

Lynmouth

Minehead

← Taw Estuary

Simonsbath

Exford

Brayford

Withypool

South Molton

Rackenford

Bishop's Nympton

Dulverton

The book's title is *Johnny Kingdom's Wild Exmoor* but where exactly is Johnny's Exmoor? An odd question but one that needs some explanation. Many people will have their own idea of what constitutes Exmoor and Johnny Kingdom is no exception. His notion of it is not constrained by the boundaries drawn up by those who planned the National Park, which came into existence in 1954, so some of the locations in this book are well beyond Exmoor as defined on the Ordnance Survey Map. The National Park, two thirds of which is in Somerset and one third in Devon, covers 265 sq mi of upland, moor, coast and woodland. In turn, that 1954 definition of Exmoor was considerably more extensive than the bounds of Exmoor Forest, not a wooded area but an unproductive wasteland, first described in Saxon times and formally designated a royal hunting ground reserved for the king after the 1066 Norman Conquest. Even the area covered by the Forest itself changed over time; parts of it were dis-afforested in agreements made with landowners and farmers. It had shrunk considerably by the time it was eventually sold off in 1818 (an early initiative in privatisation) to a Worcestershire iron-master called John Knight.

So Exmoor has always been something of a moveable feast. Within broad limits, it has become what the lover of the place wants it to be and no one is a more faithful lover of the moor than Johnny Kingdom. Though not technically within the boundary of the National Park, Johnny's Exmoor includes Bishop's Nympton, the village in which he lives; South Molton, his local market town; Brayford, where he grew up and Rackenford, where he does a lot of wildlife filming. Johnny is a Devon man and his Exmoor includes stretches of North Devon where he films, the land he owns, his 'secret place' where he watches red deer, badgers and wild boar, the estuary of the River Torridge, where he enjoys winter days watching wading birds and even the course of the River Taw, when he is looking for otters.

On the other hand, Johnny spends little time further east. The Brendon Hills are part of the National Park but not really a part of Johnny's Exmoor. Apart from Christmas markets and the August show, neither is the tourist 'honey pot' of Dunster.

While Johnny Kingdom's sense of Exmoor may be idiosyncratic, it's really no more arbitrary than other people's, and no less enjoyable for it. To the visitor, the area is perhaps best known for its heather moorland, a vast tract of open, uncultivated, peaty uplands that display wonderfully varied hues throughout the year. Bracken marks the passing of the seasons, turning from fresh green to rich red, gold and brown; purple ling contrasts with the pink of the cross-leaved heather and bright yellow gorse. The changing colours of the broadleafed woodland in the steep valleys draw many visitors in the autumn.

Exmoor has been losing this classic moorland for generations. Losses continued even after the creation of the National Park Authority in 1954 and of a pressure group, The Exmoor Society, in 1958, both committed to preserving the distinctive 'moor' in Exmoor. Farmers continued to do what they had been doing ever since they started farming the area, enclosing parcels of moorland, then ploughing and planting permanent pasture. The fields they created bore little resemblance to the open moor that the National Park had been created to celebrate, if not protect. Today, some of the moorland is being clawed back and protected, thanks in part to agreements between farmers and agencies like Natural England and to the farming policies of the National Trust, one of the biggest landowners in the area.

All of the locations mentioned in the book can be visited and enjoyed, though they are notnecessarily on the regular tourist 'beaten track' of the moor; you won't find much here about Dunster, Lynmouth, 'Lorna Doone Country' or Dulverton. But the places I do write about are not so out of the way they are impossible to reach.

Walking is the key to it all. A few years ago someone mentioned to me a survey that had revealed the majority of visitors to Exmoor never let their car out of their sight. That is a pity because undoubtedly the best way to enjoy Exmoor is to walk it. And if, like me, you believe that one of the rewards of a walk on the moor should be a decent cup of tea, I hope that some of the tea shops and cafes mentioned in the text will bring as much pleasure to you as they have done to me. One of the less onerous tasks of a writer is to judge the quality of the scones in a cream tea.

Researching the best places to enjoy a cream tea was all my own work, but this book would not have been possible without the help of many friends, colleagues and enthusiasts of Exmoor. Chris Chapman, Caroline Giddings and Noel Allen (alas, now deceased) were instrumental in guiding my initial interests in Exmoor's varied landscapes, while David Bawden and Kathy Stevens illuminated the complex life of the sheep farming communities on the moor. Writing about the Exmoor pony would have been impossible without the expert thoughts of Rex Milton, Valerie Sherwin and Sue McGeever, Denise Sage and Bob Looney were a mine of information about what is going on in Porlock while many people provided photographs when I could not.

The people who allowed me onto their land or into their homes to share tea, cake and conversation are too numerous to mention and I thank them all for their hospitality and patience. I am also grateful to friends and family who read the draft manuscript. They all made helpful (and sometimes not so helpful) suggestions and comments: Wendy McLean, Louis Parker, Adrian Bailey, Becky Lisle, Peter Symes, Colin Thomas, and, finally, Jenni Mills, who went through the manuscript with a fine-tooth comb and a very sharp pencil. As is always the case, the opinions expressed in the text are the author's alone, as is the responsibility for any errors.

But top of my list of thank-yous are three people: Wendy McLean who directed the television series and gave me the support I needed to write the book that accompanies it and Johnny and Julie Kingdom. Johnny knows Exmoor like the back of his hand and from our first meeting his hand has been instrumental in setting me on the right track. Luckily, Julie knows Johnny like the back of her hand and her support has been invaluable from the beginning. Thanks to all three of them.

1. Mr Kingdom, I Presume

IT WAS IN THE spring of 1996 that Johnny Kingdom came into my life. I remember the occasion only too well. My first encounter with the man was in the pretty village of Wheddon Cross where I was shooting a sequence for a film about wild red deer, the ruby in Exmoor's crown, about how they lived and how they died. To show the latter, I wanted to include a sequence about stag hunting.

I was intrigued by hunting and the rituals that accompany it. At that time, South West England was the only place in Britain where people hunted and killed red deer with packs of hounds. I had hoped, naively as it turned out, that I would be able to shoot the end of a hunt and the death of a deer with the help of the largest of the three stag hunts in the area, The Devon and Somerset Staghounds. I had asked permission to follow a 'meet' taking place at Wheddon Cross.

It was a bitterly cold morning but clear and crisp. The sky was a deep blue and Dunkery Beacon, the highest point in Somerset, provided a dramatic backdrop to one of the classic scenes of the English countryside. The hunt was meeting just outside the village.

Johnny was at the 'meet' with his video camera. He was curious about me but at the same time extremely suspicious. I can understand why. He was a local man, with Exmoor's blood running through his veins, on his home patch, filming an Exmoor tradition he knew inside out. I on the other hand was an outsider, a man from the city, a film maker who confessed to knowing next to nothing about the practice I was hoping to film. And hunting is one of the most controversial aspects of countryside culture. No wonder he was wary. When I told him I hoped to film both the hunt and the kill, he uttered only two words: 'No chance.'

He was right. Filming hunting's rituals at the meet was easy: the bowler-hatted members of the hunt on horseback, the followers quaffing tots of whisky, the officials in hunting pink, the hounds circling, keen and excited. But the rest of the day was a nightmare. After the whisky and the chat, the huntsman led off, the rest of the hunt on horseback trailing in a long line like a procession. At the back came the four-wheel drive followers.

The two leading hounds, the tufters, flushed the deer from cover. Then the rest of the pack were released and set off in full cry, an exhilarating sight. The hunt had been kind enough to give me a

Ready for the off – hunters gather at Exford
LOUIS PARKER

Johnny and Julie in the '80s – with hair styles to match
JOHNNY KINGDOM

guide, a local auctioneer called Tom Rook. But after hours of driving and stumbling across moor we never came anywhere near the kill.

My day's filming had ended in abject failure so on a hot afternoon in April 1996 I found myself on the road towards the village on the edge of the moor where Johnny lives, to ask for his help in getting the shots I needed to complete my programme.

Our encounter at the meet had been so brief that I was uncertain as to how we might get on but when I pulled up outside his home I was a little reassured. Johnny and his wife Julie still live in what was once a council house on the edge of Bishop's Nympton. It's the type of well-tended estate found on the outskirts of many English villages, a reminder that rural grandees were prepared to have working folk living close but not *too* close, to the heart of their domain. The Kingdom house was remarkably similar to the one in which I myself had grown up. It was as tidy and well-tended; a Rayburn kept the kitchen warm.

Julie welcomed me with a smile and a Victoria sponge cake. I don't know if she had baked it especially for me but it was delicious. I glanced up to see the *Dairy Book of Home Cookery* on a shelf. I have the same book in my kitchen; it all helped me feel at home.

Johnny was still cautious. He wanted to know my motives, why I wanted to make a film about hunting, why I wanted him to help, and he kept impressing on me why there was no chance I could make the film I wanted to. It was the man of the countryside putting the urban interloper in his place. But slowly he began to talk and I soon discovered what a complex man he is: highly intelligent, yet with little formal education; sharp and witty, yet naïve; kind-hearted yet self-obsessed... but above all, strong-willed and resolute.

Not a big man, Johnny is around 5'7" tall. He is thick set, stocky with a vice-like handshake. His hands are covered in tattoos, a legacy from his days of National Service. He has sharp, questioning, grey-blue eyes and wavy hair, a moustache and a cocked-head smile. What sets him apart however is the way he dresses: his camouflage gear. On anyone else it might look faintly ridiculous; on Johnny it looks perfect. It's not hard to imagine that he was born wearing it. Heavy boots, camouflage-patterned trousers, green polo shirt under a heavy camouflage jacket, topped off with his signature hat.

The hat is the crowning glory. It could not be more a part of Johnny if it were physically attached to him. There are always a few pheasant feathers in the band and a collection of badges, some given to him by enthusiasts. Reading the badges is a way of exploring his character, as a palmist might read the open hand. They reveal a lot about the places he's been to, the organizations with which he's had dealings, the people he's met.

These days the gear may be more expensive than it was when I first met him but the hat has never changed, which is comforting. He wears variations of this uniform at home, on his land, in his local pub: everywhere in fact. It is a calling card and passport rolled into one. Could anyone else get away with it? I doubt it.

Apart from his dress and his voice, Johnny's other signature is his vehicle. Unlike the hat the truck has changed over time. When I first met him he had an old Mitsubishi with plenty of Exmoor clay daubed inside and out. Adorned with signs, pictures and telephone numbers, it was a constant, if uncomfortable, reminder of his day-to-day activity. Plumbers' vans advertise plumbing services, Johnny's truck marketed a wildlife service.

These days he drives a much more upmarket version. On his current vehicle the camouflage paint is an all-over job. It's so effective I've found it hard to find him out on the moor. Inside, it's extremely comfortable and I'm sure easier to drive but somehow I miss the old truck. It felt part of Johnny.

Johnny suitably attired
WENDY McLEAN

If the hat fits – wear it

It was the old truck that was parked outside the house on that day in April 1996 when Johnny, dressed inevitably in camouflage, began to recount his life story. He was born in 1939 just up the road from Brayford, a quarry village in North Devon. He left school with no qualifications and, after National Service, during which he was in constant trouble with the authorities, held down

15

The church of All Saints – High Bray

My first video camera

various jobs in the local quarry and in Exmoor's woodlands, before becoming a gravedigger.

After we'd finished Julie's tea and cake, Johnny took me into a little room at the back of the house, next to the lavatory, which he had converted into an office, storeroom and video-editing suite. We squeezed into the cramped space, full of camera equipment and old video cases, with antlers hanging from the walls amid photographs of him and his family and his wildlife. He showed me some of the thousands of video shots of red deer he had amassed over the years.

It was a strange and wonderfully bizarre collection, quite unlike anything I had witnessed before. He had begun filming wildlife after a serious accident had left him unable to work. A friend had given him a camera to help him recuperate emotionally and psychologically. The gift had changed his life. He used the video camera like no one I had ever seen.

He broke all the rules of filming. He tried to film wildlife close up, without a tripod so some of his shots wobbled like a jelly. He used the zoom and pan functions too often, trying to edit the video as he was shooting it, a mistake no professional wildlife cameraman would ever make and he talked over the pictures, incessantly. But none of this seemed to matter because Johnny's filming had one amazing quality I had never come across in anyone else's work.

It created an intimate relationship with the wildlife he was observing. He really did talk to the animals through his camera and it made for compelling viewing. When you watched his film of a deer stalk, a blackbird sitting on eggs, or fox cubs poking their heads above ground for the first time, you had the feeling that you were there with him, out on the moor or deep in the woodland, living the moment and sharing a unique experience. That, for me, was and remains Johnny Kingdom's greatest gift.

I never did find out if Johnny had filmed the end to the day's hunting. He wouldn't say and looking back, I don't blame him, it would have caused him more trouble than it was worth. In any case, after he had spent hours showing me the quality of the wildlife video he did have, the question of hunting faded into insignificance.

Here was an absolute treasure trove of images of Exmoor that I was sure would make compelling television. After all, if I had been gripped by Johnny's skill and enthusiasm, why would others feel differently?

I was convinced, but I needed to persuade other people in the business to feel the same way and get Johnny and his films onto television. I thought it would be easy. I was wrong.

It took me three years to find someone with power in television who agreed with me about Johnny's unique abilities. In that time, I wrote to commissioning editors, the people who decide what will be on the screen, at the BBC, ITV, Channel 4 and Channel 5. No one was interested. None of them could see the potential in Johnny's personality and his video. When someone left or was promoted, or sacked, I wrote to their successor. I made taster tapes, wrote different proposals for different approaches, all to no avail. Then one day in February 1999 I had a breakthrough that changed my life and Johnny's.

*Winter sun at The London Inn
Molland*

*Footprints in the
mud – a red deer stag*

I had been talking about him to the Head of Factual Programmes at the regional ITV channel, HTV, urging her to meet him and to my astonishment she eventually agreed. She'd seen his amateur videos and was none too impressed but she liked Exmoor and she liked my company's work. So on a bitterly cold but bright February morning, Sandra Jones and I drove together to meet Johnny for lunch at The London Inn, one of my favourite pubs on the moor and to search for deer.

This was our chance, perhaps our last chance and I knew we could not afford to fail. Johnny and I had planned the trip meticulously. While we drove down from Bristol, he was out on the moor looking for deer.

After lunch in front of a roaring fire, Johnny took us on a deer stalk. We made our way through gorse bushes onto a track on the edge of a wood. Johnny used all his field craft and intimate knowledge of the area to show her the habitat of the red deer. He stopped and pointed to the footprints, the 'slots', that different deer make in the ground.

The slots were fresh. Would that mean there were deer about? He showed her deer droppings and how they were different from sheep and rabbit droppings. He showed her the 'racks' where deer moved across steep-sided lanes from field to woodland. We walked and talked quietly for about an hour. Eventually the narrow track we were following opened up. On one side was a traditional Exmoor bank made of earth and stone with beech trees on top.

Johnny became animated and suggested we should be very quiet. He crawled slowly up the bank and peered over the top, then beckoned us to follow. As Sandra's head bobbed above the tufts of grass on top of the bank, I don't think she could believe her eyes. There, in the field about 25 yards away, was a herd of thirty red deer females, hinds. Busy munching grass, they had not noticed us at all. Sandra had never seen a red deer in her life. She was ecstatic and so were we. We knew then that Johnny would get his first series on television.

Johnny Kingdom's Wild West was transmitted on HTV in the spring of 2000. The programmes broke audience records and a second series followed the following year. We were on our way.

I know you are there –
a hind in winter
JOHNNY KINGDOM

PART ONE
WINTER

2. Big Plans and Grand Designs
Johnny's Winter

THIS IS ONE OF the classic picture-postcard scenes of winter on Exmoor, a carpet of snow on one of the high moors and it is certainly the case that Exmoor gets more snow than many other parts of England. Encouraged by the strong south westerly winds, no sooner has it snowed than the narrow roads on the top of the moor can become blocked by drifts.

If only every winter's day on Exmoor could be like this. Sadly, much more common is rain and Exmoor rain is something else.

The Barle Valley in November – wet

Previous page: *Winter on West Anstey Common*

The Barle Valley in January – snow
JO DOWN

You should have been here yesterday – Johnny looking for wildlife in the rain

And finding it JOHNNY KINGDOM

Exmoor rain has the habit of penetrating even the most durable outdoor clothing. Whipped up by westerly winds, it can drive hard, soaking the hardiest walker or wildlife enthusiast in a freezing blanket. It has something to do with Exmoor's location. Looking west, there is nothing except thousands of miles of the Atlantic. Clouds pick up water from the ocean and when they arrive in Britain they deposit their contents on the first high land they hit, the moorlands of South West Britain.

Exmoor rain is more often than not accompanied by low cloud and mist. The effect is twofold: it makes it much more difficult to watch wildlife and the rain gets right into the bones. Not the most pleasant experience.

Johnny, growing up in this sort of weather, seems impervious to it. He wears his coat and collar open, as if challenging the heavens to pour more water over him because, as he'd put it: 'It won't make no effect.'

It was on such a frustrating, disappointing Exmoor winter day in November 2013 that I persuaded some of the ITV network commissioning team to come to Exmoor to meet Johnny. By now he had appeared on national BBC television and on UKTV. But ITV had always seemed to me his natural home.

I was hoping we could repeat the successful formula that had won him his first television series more than a decade ago. I longed for another of those crystal blue, bitterly cold winter days when you can see your breath. What we got was rain, rain in the morning, rain at lunchtime and rain in the afternoon. It was raining when we met Johnny and it was still raining when we left him. We lowered our expectations to a distant glimpse of a red deer, maybe a couple of Exmoor ponies

Top: *The intrepid band of brothers (and sister)*

Above: *Johnny in intense negotiations with Wendy McLean the series director. They decided on the Corn Dolly tea shop in South Molton*

looking as miserable as we felt and, if we were very lucky, a bedraggled bird of prey or two.

Not that the rain bothered Johnny. His enthusiasm for Exmoor and its wildlife is boundless, never dampened by inclement weather. After the regulation kiss (with the women, not me) we sped off in his truck in search of something to impress the young commissioning executives. And he did not disappoint. Even in the worst of the driving rain and swirling mist below Dunkery Beacon, Johnny was able to find a couple of deer grazing in the fields. It was a triumph of persistence over adversity and impressed the young women down from London no end, just as it had impressed others in the past. They were smitten. Johnny was going to be back on ITV, this time nationally. The plan was to start filming for the series in January 2014.

Winter for most of us is a quiet period, a time to take stock after Christmas and get ready for the year ahead. Not for Johnny: for him, winter is a busy time, or at least it was in 2014. Not only was he almost fully occupied filming Exmoor's winter wildlife, he was planning a major project on the land he and Julie own.

The land in question is 50 or so acres they bought in 2006, part meadow, part stream, marsh and pond and part broadleaved woodland. An impressive collection of animals and birds live mainly in the woodland: deer, foxes, badgers, wild boar, woodpeckers, owls and any number of woodland song birds. He also has otters, herons and hares visiting. It's a paradise of sorts, a sanctuary to which he can escape when the pressures of everyday living get too much. He has an impressive array of gadgets that allow him to film in this sanctuary: remote cameras in bird boxes, hides looking over the pond and dotted around the woodland and places where he can watch the animal residents and visitors to his land as they rest up or feed.

For Johnny, buying the land was a liberation. Before then his wildlife filming was dependent on the goodwill of a few Exmoor farmers and landowners. Some, like his longtime friend, Tony Thorne at Twitchen, a farming family at Anstey called the Miltons, and Roger Gregory, the man who first introduced Johnny to a video camera, were welcoming. They understood the sort of man Johnny is, were tolerant and helpful and the result was some wonderful film of barn owls, fox cubs, ponies, badgers and red deer. Others were less tolerant; a number hostile. They had made life difficult for him even on the open moorland where others seemed to be free to roam and film with impunity. But once he and Julie owned their own patch of land, he became free from the constant hassle and has used freedom to the full. He is there every spare minute of every day; midwinter is no different from midsummer and there is never a time when he does not have some project on the go.

Winter 2014 saw him embark on one of his most ambitious so far. Badgers are probably Johnny's favourite wild animal. He has spent years watching them and has gone further than most to observe their behaviour.

Now he wanted to build an underground chamber where badgers could live and rear their young, a sett in which he could rig cameras to record the whole process, something he had never before attempted. Time, however, was not on his side. Badgers have their young in January or February so

Johnny and Julie's land in winter

Top: *'Tigger and Owl' – Johnny with his mate Bob Sampson*
WENDY McLEAN

Above: *Modest beginnings for the Grand Design – the badger house*
RUPERT SMITH

he would need to complete the structure very quickly to have any prospect of fulfilling his ambition.

Badgers like digging and Johnny was going to have to behave like them. He would need to dig and dig deep. And because it was all going to happen in January he would have to dig in the rain, in Exmoor rain, indeed in the worst rain Exmoor had experienced for a generation.

The plan was to dig into the side of a valley on his land where he knew badgers had existing setts and into which he would sink some sort of container. He would need help so he turned to the man who had assisted him with all sorts of technical problems in the past, Bob Sampson. Bob is the perfect foil to Johnny's hyperactive approach to life. He is calmness personified, a reflective, phlegmatic Exmoor soul with understated humour and a knowing look. Bob is 'Owl' to the 'Tigger' that is Johnny.

To say that Bob is good with a screwdriver is like saying Mary Berry is handy with a whisk. In the past he has helped Johnny with projects as varied as cameras fixed branch-high in trees to film woodpeckers at their nest and remote-controlled miniature vehicles to venture into badger setts. But to build a badger chamber underground and rig it with tunnels and cameras would be their biggest challenge by far.

Luckily, Bob is the sort who likes a challenge. He did not disappoint. He had just the home for Johnny's badgers, though not the sort of home that might appeal to you or me. Bob had a septic tank.

On a rain soaked morning in January, Johnny met Bob at his workshop to pick up the tank. Johnny was sceptical. A septic tank was not quite what he had in mind for his winter Grand Design. And this septic tank did not even look much like a conventional tank. It was ball shaped, like something that could have featured in *Twenty Thousand Leagues Under the Sea*. Bob, ever the optimist, was convinced it would work. He even had ideas about where the tunnels, the front and back door, and the sleeping accommodation should be located. Kevin McCleod would have been proud of him. Reluctantly, Johnny went along with his mate and together they lifted the new badger home-to-be onto a pickup truck for the journey to Johnny's land.

Bob had put a lot of thought into the new home. He had designed it with all the mod cons any prospective badger tenant might need. It came with a door at the front, a tradesman's entrance at the rear and various mezzanine floors where the occupants of this most desirable residence could find a little privacy. For his part, Johnny had thought long and hard about the interior design. Hay and straw were part of the furnishings and the whole sett was to be wired for sound and video, for Johnny's benefit rather than the residents'.

All through a wet January, Johnny laboured on the new sett in a quagmire of mud. He and Bob placed the tank in what they considered to be the ideal position and then laid the tunnels, pieces of 12 inch diameter plastic drain pipe, until finally the cameras were rigged and Johnny's grand design was ready for occupation.

Would the badgers move in? No one, least of all Johnny, knew. Using one of his favourite expressions, all he could do now was wait.

3. The Jewel in Exmoor's Crown – Red Deer

WHEN YOU DRIVE to Exmoor, you know that you have reached the boundary of the National Park because you are greeted by a roadside stone emblazoned with its symbol, a set of red deer antlers. And once inside the Park, you are never allowed to forget that Exmoor is home to this most beautiful animal.

It might be one of smallest of the National Parks but Exmoor has more red deer than anywhere else in the whole of England or Wales. Three thousand roam the moor. They have been part of Johnny's life for as long as he can remember.

Red deer were the first animals he filmed and he's filmed them in all seasons and in every type of weather. He's been almost frozen to death, swept off his feet in the strong south-westerlies and drenched like a drowned rat. But it's always been worth it because for Johnny there is no finer sight on Exmoor than a stag with its hinds, roaring at the top of its voice, or 'bolving' as it's known locally.

Welcome to Exmoor

A hind and her calf
JOHNNY KINGDOM

The red deer is Britain's biggest mammal. Stags can grow to a height of between three and five feet to the shoulder and weigh anything up to two hundred pounds. Hinds, the females, are smaller, growing to around two to four feet. Calves are born in early summer, one year old deer are known as yearlings and those in their second year are called 'pricketts', though as Johnny says: 'You have to be careful how you say that, especially if there are ladies about.' Red deer live in separate herds of hinds and stags and come together only in the autumn mating season.

Watching the red deer

Along with Exmoor ponies, the chance of spotting red deer is one of the most popular reasons for visits to the area. But they are never easy to track or see. Johnny has some sound advice about field craft for anyone wanting to get close to the deer.

This is how Johnny will dress when he is looking for deer. It's not always necessary to go as far as a mask and full camouflage but it is advisable not to wear bright colours. Deer do not have brilliant eyesight so wearing autumn hues, greens and browns, will go some way to prevent them spotting the enthusiastic amateur. Approaching slowly, with no sudden movements, also helps.

It's best to stalk from the correct direction. Deer have a superb sense of smell so it's important to have the wind in your face as you near the quarry. If the wind is behind you they will smell you and move on.

Knowing the habits of the animals is always useful if you want to see them at close quarters, or film or photograph them. They are easiest to find in the early morning or late afternoon when they are feeding. Johnny's advice is, crucially, not to be in too much of a hurry. When he's out stalking he starts early in the morning and is prepared to wait, often in a thicket or beside a big tree trunk, for hours: 'If you are patient, the deer will come to you.'

Winter

Winters on Exmoor can be very hard but red deer have just the outfit to cope; a superb, thick, warm coat that becomes even thicker round the neck, like a big collar or scarf. During harsh weather they spend a lot of time sheltering in woods but it's still possible see them out on the moor looking for food. They might make their way slowly across the moorland, one behind the other, like a caravan of camels.

One of the best times to see deer is after a fall of snow. Framed against a white background, their tracks, or slots, show up well in the snow so it's relatively easy to follow them. Nevertheless it's still important to remember your field craft. Humans stand out against a white background every bit as starkly as do deer!

A 'wallow' is also a good place to watch deer and Johnny has often successfully filmed at such a spot.

Ready for action

Opposite: *There's no finer sight on Exmoor – a mature red deer stag and his hinds*
JOHNNY KINGDOM

The rewards of hours of stalking
JOHNNY KINGDOM

Bath time in a wallow
JOHNNY KINGDOM

A wallow is a big mud pit, sometimes also known as a 'soiling pit'. Wallows tend to be tucked away in woodland; they are the deer's equivalent of a bathroom and they like a bit of privacy! The big difference from a human bathroom is that the wallow is filled with mud rather than water. Deer use wallows to clean themselves and particularly to remove ticks from their coats. A stag will approach the wallow rather like a man might approach a bathroom: with extreme caution. He'll scent the ground and if the wallow is already occupied he might even wait his turn, though the wait will not be as long as that often suffered by a male unfortunate enough to find the bathroom occupied by a female of the human species.

And once a deer knows the wallow, it will come back time and time again. Having waited its turn, it will then lie down in the wallow, rolling over and over to cover its coat with mud. Think of youngsters at a wet Glastonbury Festival and you will get the picture.

28

Spring

Watching red deer in the spring is a very different experience from watching in winter. Spring is a lovely time on the moor. New grass and shoots are coming through and there is plenty of food for the deer. They need it; they look their worst at the end of a hard winter.

It was at this time of year, the back end of winter turning to the beginning of spring, when Johnny and I first met at the stag hunt. Hunting deer has been part of Exmoor life since the time of the Normans and when I think back to the day I met Johnny at the meet, what I remember most strongly was the feeling of having somehow stepped back in time.

For Johnny, hunting, whatever he thinks of it, is part of the warp and weft of the countryside in which he grew up.

The arguments for and against hunting deer on Exmoor continue – and so do the deer, through their yearly cycle. By March hinds are carrying calves, while stags are losing their antlers. A set of antlers is a prize for people who comb the combes to collect them. When he's not in his workshop in South Molton, Mike Fook, a good friend of Johnny's, spends hours looking for antlers just for the love of it.

Left: *What you see at stag hunts*

Below: *What you don't see at stag hunts* JOHNNY KINGDOM

Mike Fook – engineer and collector

Right: Tom Lock's workshop – Hawkridge

Below: What went wrong? A prize-winning distorted antler

There will always be plenty for Mike to collect because stags regrow their antlers every summer. New ones begin to bud soon after the old ones have been discarded. In the early stages they are covered in what is known as 'velvet', tiny membranes of blood vessels with a soft smooth texture exactly like velvet material.

There's an old wives tale that says a red deer's antlers grow in time with the bracken on the moor and Johnny thinks there's a lot in that.

A young stag does not grow any antlers at all in his first year. In the second, when he is a prickett, he grows two 'uprights' or unbranched antlers. Then in subsequent years, the stag will grow a spur or 'point' on the antlers. In the third year, he grows what is known as a 'brow point', (easily memorable if you think of your eyebrow). In the following year he adds a 'bey' point, then the year after that a 'trey' point.

When he has three points, Exmoor people say: 'He's got all his rights and three atop,' and is now a 'royal' stag.

However, some of the strangely twisted and distorted antlers in Mike's collection bear little resemblance to the standard pattern. He believes these may have been damaged in some way,

All his rights and three atop – a royal stag
JOHNNY KINGDOM

Tom Lock – now

Tom Lock – then
TOM LOCK ARCHIVE

perhaps on a stone or a tree trunk. Although he collects primarily for fun, Mike likes to enter his finds into competitions. The rosettes he has won show just how successful he's been. One specimen, on display in his shop, won first prize in the category of 'Most Unusual-shaped Antler' at the Exford Show in July 2014.

Mike enjoys just collecting antlers for display and fun but others go much further. In the delightfully unspoiled village of Hawkridge, another old acquaintance of Johnny's, Tom Lock, has a workshop where he fashions chairs, stools, walking sticks, candle sticks and even toggles for zips from deer antler. His workshop is like a place that time forgot. Light from the window spills in on rows of tools rarely seen these days. In the far corner sits Tom, like a craftsman from a bygone age, though the electric light bulb is something of a giveaway.

In spite of pushing ninety, Tom is there most days of the week. His family have owned the workshop in the village for generations. He can trace his wheelwright antecedents back to 1840, though by the time Tom had learned to make a wooden cartwheel wagons were disappearing fast and tractors coming in.

The workshop is easy to find, opening onto the only road running through the village. Tom sells his products directly from it, eliminating the middle man; he welcomes passers-by and he has time to chat as he works. It's a scene that has all but vanished from today's countryside so visit him while there is still time and don't forget to carry cash. Not altogether surprisingly, he doesn't take credit cards.

Summer

Whilst summer is a busy time for red deer stags growing new antlers it is also a crucial time of the year for the females: their calves are born. A hind ready to give birth will leave the rest of the herd to find a quiet spot to have her baby. With small white marks on their backs, calves look especially endearing, when they take their first faltering steps they are often not even as tall as the grass concealing them.

June and July are popular with walkers on the moor and it's possible, though rare, to stumble across a calf. If you are lucky enough to come across one, Johnny's advice is: 'Never touch it. If the mother smells you on the baby's body she might abandon it and it will die. Be very quiet, just take a look, then move away.'

A newborn deer calf is extremely vulnerable and it is well known that one particular injured calf was very special to Johnny. It was in 1994 when he found her caught on a fence, just a few days old. Most people would have put down a calf with an injured leg but Johnny is not most people. He rescued her, then reared her after a vet had amputated the injured leg. Bambi survived until July 2006, remarkable for a deer with only three legs.

Stags in velvet
JOHNNY KINGDOM

Johnny and Roger's Bambi
JOHNNY KINGDOM

Where's my mum? – A solitary calf
JOHNNY KINGDOM

Johnny and Bambi
WENDY McLEAN

But his close encounters with red deer calves go back further. An old friend, Roger Gregory, has been an important figure in Johnny's life for all sorts of reasons. Johnny's career as a wildlife videographer is down to Roger. When he had a serious accident, caught between the hydraulic arm of a tractor and a group of mature oak trees, it was Roger who loaned him a video camera to help him recuperate. The rest, as they say, is history.

'Johnny was a bit of a jack the lad, still is,' Roger recalls, 'but his heart was always in the right place.'

Roger and his Bambi

It was more than thirty years ago, the second week in June, when Johnny and Roger found a new born red deer calf. The two of them were out together filming wildlife when they came across the calf. It was very young, young enough to still have the membrane from birth on its body. They were concerned about the welfare of the newborn but left it alone, expecting the mother to come back for its baby. When they returned to the spot the following day, you can imagine their consternation to see that the calf was still there, alone, abandoned. When they attempted to leave for the second time, the calf was having none of it, it followed them. They still are not sure which one of them it mistook for its mother but it was Roger who held the orphan while Johnny drove them back to Roger's place.

The two of them nursed the newborn calf as if it was one of their children. They stayed up at night, feeding it goat's milk using a baby's bottle. Johnny built her a shed for shelter.

That deer too was christened Bambi. (Those people of Exmoor who are generous enough to rescue abandoned deer really do need to show a bit more imagination in naming them.) As Roger's Bambi grew, he took her for walks with his dog.

'Until she began to develop a mind of her own,' he says. 'Then I had to stop it. I remember one time when she lay down in the middle of the rugby pitch and we could not move her. She'd gone into town for a look around!'

But he reckons that as she has become older, she has mellowed. Bambi 1 lives in a pen on Roger's land. Of course, people said the relationship wouldn't last. That was more than thirty years ago. Roger thinks his deer might well see him out!

Out on the moor, while the hinds are rearing calves, the heady mix of purple and mauve of the flowering heathers and the brilliant yellow of gorse is the climax to the summer. Stags are ridding themselves of the last shreds of 'velvet', the blood vessel membranes, from their antlers. As the antlers grow and mature, the blood vessels dry and wither. It's possible to see fragments of velvet hanging loose from antlers, like socks drying on a washing line.

Autumn

Towards the end of September antlers are once more fully grown and the velvet gone. For most people who know Exmoor the favourite time to look for red deer is in the autumn, against a

Top: *Contestants fighting for the prize*
JOHNNY KINGDOM

Above: *To the victor the spoils*
JOHNNY KINGDOM

spectacular backdrop of colours with the woodland and moor a brilliant mix of browns, reds and golds.

Autumn is a good time to watch deer because it is their mating, or rutting season; during the rut stags tend to be pre-occupied and less concerned about people watching them. On the other hand, this is the one time of the year when a stag might be dangerous. During the 2014 rutting season in Scotland a woman was gored to death by a stag. So it is best to be careful and not attempt to get too close. Johnny himself has had quite a few close shaves.

One incident occurred during filming for one of our television programmes, while he was tracking a mature stag. We had been following Johnny stalking for a couple of hours and it was beginning to get dark. He wanted to get a really good shot of this big stag on his own camera while we wanted to film him getting it.

He followed the stag quietly through some gorse, advising us to hold back, it would be easier on his own. He was right. As he tracked the stag he moved closer and closer until he was almost within touching distance. He thought he was safe but then, quite suddenly, the roaring stag turned and came towards him. It was as if it was saying: 'Right mate, I've just about had enough of you.'

I've never seen Johnny quite so scared. His first impulse was to run, as was the camera crew's but that is the worst thing you can do when a stag turns on you. Instead, Johnny stood quite still. I could tell he was absolutely petrified because he was wearing a radio microphone which picked up the sound of his heart thumping at what seemed like twice the usual rate. In other circumstances it would have been amusing but the last thing any of us were doing on that autumn late afternoon was laughing.

The stag strutted closer and closer, so close that Johnny could almost touch the beast. Then, when we all thought he was in serious trouble, it moved on past him. A surge of adrenalin and relief washed over us all and the microphones picked up a few choice expletives. He'd had a lucky escape. But – and this is the sheer joy of filming – Johnny had been so preoccupied with the stag that he'd kept his video camera running throughout the incident and filmed a shot of it up very close. Brilliant and very fortunate.

Such aggression is typical of the behaviour of a stag wanting to protect his hinds during the rutting season. It is part of the competition between stags; mature males have to fight off young pretenders to defend their harem. Sometimes you can hear the clashing of antlers as they go head to head. This behaviour can go on for an hour or so while the hinds stand back, calmly carrying on grazing, as if they are contemptuous of the juvenile antics they are witnessing. But when one stag has finally won the battle, he'll enjoy the prize of mating with all the hinds in the harem. If he loses, a new stag takes over the group. That's wildlife for you.

When in late autumn the rut is finally over, stags and hinds go their separate ways once again, to survive the long, wet winter and, if they're lucky, the pursuing hunt.

4. The Moor in Winter

WINTER MAY NOT seem like the best time of the year to appreciate Exmoor's landscape and wildlife but there are some real advantages to seeing the moor uncluttered by foliage, bracken or people. The Bronze Age barrows on the southern ridge, the humps and bumps of lost medieval villages along Badgworthy Water, or the stark outline of the beech hedges that have been ignored and allowed to grow unchecked are just some of the highlights of the landscape best appreciated in the depths of winter.

Baby it's cold outside – Exmoor ponies untroubled by the snow
JOHNNY KINGDOM

A thrush picnics outside Johnny's house
JOHNNY KINGDOM

What is true for the landscape is true also for its wildlife. Some animals will have disappeared from the scene: badgers tucked away in their setts, dormice hibernating, swallows and swifts headed for warmer climates. But foxes will venture out for food, there are numerous birds about in woods, on rivers and on the coast, and winter is a terrific time to watch red deer. The sight of a line of stags, walking slowly across the open moorland in driving rain or snow, is one of the most uplifting sights Exmoor affords.

The coast in winter

The coast is especially attractive at this time of year and a great place to see birds. Two locations bookend the area. To the east are the marshes at Dunster Hawn at the mouth of the River Avill, while further west is the estuary of the Rivers Taw and Torridge. Both are havens for winter bird life, with tidal coast and estuary mud banks rich in the sort of food waders love.

Fremington Quay

The estuary of the Taw, on the B3233 Barnstaple to Instow road, is one of Johnny's favourite places to film winter waders and migrants. Fremington Quay is reached easily by road or cycle path from Barnstaple. The ideal time to be there is as the tide goes out, when a variety of waders feed on the sand and mud. On almost any day you can see: curlews, egrets, and perhaps spoon bills, as well as small groups of oyster catchers or dunlin. It is possible to sit tucked up against the rock face, close to the spot where an old disused railway line crosses Fremington Creek and just wait for the birds to come to you.

Not that it was quite as easy as that when I pitched up with Johnny to film on a crystal clear February morning in 2014.

The day had started well enough. I was there bright and early, waiting for Johnny and Rupert Smith, our cameraman, to arrive. The weather forecast was spot on, the early morning tide was high and the day promised a lot. Then Johnny arrived. I was expecting a hearty greeting, what I received was a volley of none-too-polite invective. He had been filming the journey down the creek from the front of his truck and because I had been standing there it had ruined the shot. A 'good' start to the day? We did the shot again, this time me hiding behind a handily located bush.

Next, while we were waiting for the tide to turn, we attempted some pieces-to-camera. Pieces-to-camera, or PTCs, are among the most difficult challenges for any television presenter: the moment of truth when the presenter has to look right into the camera lens and talk to the audience as if he or she were having a one-to-one conversation, without getting tongue-tied, losing the thread of what they are saying, or falling over their own feet. Over the years, Johnny had become a master of the technique.

However, most presenters I've worked with have problems with PTCs from time to time and Johnny is no different. Unfortunately this was one of those times. He just could not get it right

The team at work – at last

and we over-ran. We were at the PTCs for a couple of hours and now the tide had turned and was on the ebb. The North Devon tidal range is enormous and the tide going out of the Taw Estuary is just like a plug being pulled from a basin. We'd arrived early, to be in plenty of time for it to turn but now we were in a rush to film before the basin emptied.

Above left: *Breakfast at Fremington*

Above right: *A curlew takes a break from feeding*

Nothing seemed to go right. We stole past the lime kilns, keeping low, hoping to get close to some oystercatchers busy gorging themselves on the molluscs left in the mud as the sea retreated. We were very quiet, but every time we approached they took fright. Then we saw a solitary egret perched on a rock, revealed as the water levels dropped. Johnny and the cameraman decided to head for it and sure enough, off it flew. We knew then we would need to be patient.

Of course, patience eventually paid off. The egret returned, the oystercatchers performed. We heard the call of a curlew and then spotted one as it feasted on the water's edge. Johnny reflected that you used to see curlews flying over the moor in summer but not these days. A solitary cormorant skimmed across the retreating tide like a silent fighter plane. A small flock of dunlin swooped over our heads, heading up the creek.

Johnny sat quietly through it all, framing the pictures, focusing and shooting the scene that unfolded before him while Rupert, equally quietly and efficiently, filmed Johnny. Eventually the pieces-to-camera flowed and Johnny had no problem conveying the sheer joy and excitement of what was before his eyes. It was the perfect illustration of his natural talent as a television performer, making you feel you are right there with him, witnessing the best of the Westcountry's wildlife in his company.

These are sights anyone with a decent map, a pair of binoculars and some patience can enjoy and if, after a few hours birdwatching, you fancy warming up with a tea or coffee, there is just the place, only yards away.

Fremington Quay Café is located in a building that was once part of the railway station, on the line from Barnstaple to Instow. Run by Charlotte Lock and her partner, it is open 363 days a year so it's really bad luck, or bad planning, if the only days you can get there are Christmas or Boxing Day.

Born and bred in North Devon, Charlotte took on the lease of the Café in 2011. The atmosphere is friendly, the food local, the cakes huge and the cream tea more than filling. And if you are one of those dedicated souls who worries that a break for lunch or a cream tea is a distraction from the serious pursuit of knowledge, fear not; there is much more to the café than just food and drink. The café has a museum and interpretation centre where you can brief yourself about the history of Fremington.

The village and quay took off in the early nineteenth century when the silting up of the River Taw had made it almost impossible for ships to use Barnstaple. Trade on the river stagnated until some enterprising entrepreneurs found a solution. They saw Fremington as an alternative port, built a quay and, in 1838, established the Taw Valley Railway Company with a horse-drawn train to Barnstaple. By 1854, when steam was introduced, the quay had been extended and improved so that by the mid-nineteenth century Fremington was the busiest port between Bristol and Land's End.

Today all that is left is the bed of the railway, a bridge carrying it across the creek, some lime kilns and the café and interpretation centre housed in what was once the railway station. You can even see where the platforms once stood, a poignant reminder of what Fremington was like less than three generations ago.

Charlotte Lock takes a break

A reminder of what the quay used to be like

Dunster Beach

At the other end of Exmoor, Dunster Beach has a very different history. While the Taw Estuary and Fremington Quay were all about industry, Dunster Beach is all about leisure.

The beach is best known today for its collection of more than 250 holiday chalets. The holiday village with its green, unassuming dwellings and accompanying shop, tennis court and café, feels strangely out of place and time in modern Britain. Looking at the chalets and the antics on the beach, I'm reminded of the time when a bucket and spade, sand and sea, were all a family needed to enjoy a holiday.

The development began modestly enough with one or two chalets as a commercial enterprise undertaken by the Luttrell family in the 1920s. The Luttrells have owned Dunster Castle, most of the village and the beach for more than 600 years. The first chalet (today Number 17) was erected in 1927 but almost before the green paint had dried it had to be moved to a more discreet position, masked by trees. The problem was that it could be seen by the squire and his lady from the castle windows, ruining the aesthetics of their view across the bay. The chalets, all painted in differing shades of green, were at first rented and then sold to enthusiastic holiday makers. By the mid-1930s there were 94 dwellings, selling at £80 each. Today there are more than 250 and

Dunster Beach – summer

Dunster Hawn – winter
JON WHITE

Oystercatchers in flight

Oystercatchers at rest

buying one will set you back around £120,000.

Close to the chalets is a fresh water lake now known as the Hawn. In years gone by, Dunster Haven, on the estuary of the River Avill, was a thriving port but by the early years of the fifteenth century the port had fallen into disuse. The tides favoured Minehead, the mouth of the Avill silted up and the Hawn pool was the result.

Today there are no less than three bird habitats: the shoreline, the woodland pool at the Hawn, and the marshy fields behind it.

On any day one might spot little flocks of dunlin, ringed plover, sanderling, curlew and oystercatchers on the shore, kingfisher and water rail on the Hawn pool and little egret in the marsh fields. Further west, towards the golf links, snow buntings are regular visitors.

After a stint on the marsh or beach watching birds, you'll have earned a cup of tea, if you can find one. At Fremington on the Taw there is only one choice but it is open all year round. At Dunster there are more tea shops and restaurants than anywhere else on the moor; on a winter afternoon though, hardly any are open. Are they missing a trick?

Exmoor's beech hedges

The Exmoor coast is a delight in winter but so is the hinterland where the hedgerows come into their own.

Beech hedges are part of the DNA of the Exmoor landscape, as much as heather moorland, hogs-back cliffs, or broad-leafed woodland. But these hedges are relatively new to the moor. They were introduced in number by John Knight, the man who bought the central area of the moor, the

A cared for beech hedge

*The man who cares for them – Martin
Burnett ready for a day's work*

Royal Forest, in 1818. Beech formed part of his plan to build a wall around his new acquisition.
Strong earth banks were topped with beech saplings and, as the trees grew, the central stem or
'leader' would be cut almost through, bent over and laid on its side, then woven or plaited with
trunks from adjacent saplings to provide a strong hedge on top of the bank.

The beech hedge took off and, by the end of the century, had become a distinctive feature of
Exmoor's landscape. In spring and summer the leaves are a vibrant green, turning golden brown
in autumn and even through winter there are enough leaves left to convey a sense of warmth on
the coldest day.

The value of the hedge was that it provided a wind break and shelter for stock, penned in
effectively by the hedges. But laying the hundreds of miles of hedges was a time-consuming,
labour-intensive job, a task that had to be done with just a bill hook, axe and saw. It was done in
winter, before the sap began to rise, and a farmer would lay his hedges every ten to fifteen years.

The First World War, when labour became scarce, saw the beginning of the demise of the laid
hedge. Tractor-driven hedge trimmers became popular in the '50s and, together with the increasing
use of barbed wire, they sealed the hedges' fate. Trees in the hedges were allowed to grow unfettered
and the hedges became full of gaps, virtually useless either as shelter or field boundary.

Those keen to recreate the look of the nineteenth century Exmoor landscape have been encouraging landowners to restore these long-gone hedges. Natural England and the National Park have sometimes funded their restoration which has helped provide a living for craftsmen like Martin Burnett, one of the few people on the moor reviving the tradition.

Laying a hedge, Martin reckons, is easy if you know how. He begins by taking out 'all the rubbish', the branches and twigs that cannot be woven into the hedge. The skill comes in cutting the living wood. The uprights are known as 'sticks' and the technique of laying them, 'steeping'. When the stick is cut and laid on its side it's called a 'steeper'. 'The sticks have to be laid uphill,' Martin explains, 'because the sap in the tree won't rise and it will die if the stick is laid downhill.'

Many people, including me, thought that hedges have to be laid in winter before the sap begins to rise. Martin assures me that is an old wives' tale. 'You can do it all year round, and beech is best laid in late spring, when it's warmer. The hedge will grow more quickly.'

Martin's skill lies in the way he cuts the sticks. 'When you cut the stick, you have to make sure you don't wrinkle the skin (the bark). If you do, the steeper will stop growing. It's like crushing the veins in your arm – the blood stops flowing.'

There are fewer people laying hedges now than there were in the recent past because, according to Martin, the government stopped offering grants to landowners and farmers. There are not many people who will have a hedge laid without a grant, though a few farmers still lay hedges and have never taken a grant.

I can see why people who worry about the look of the landscape in the National Park want to get back to a time when hedges were laid but there is a beauty in a hedge that has been neglected for decades. The landscape artist Jo Down agrees. Jo has lived on Exmoor for forty years and was attracted to these strange, stark natural shapes when she first arrived. What has always fascinated her is that the seemingly natural shape of the beech trees is, paradoxically, a direct consequence of man's influence on that landscape. The technique she uses in her work to capture that paradox is exquisite: watercolours for the backgrounds, ink to bring out the striking foreground of these stark and strange features.

You can see more of Jo's work on her website: www.moorlandart.wordpress.com

Top: *A remnant of an old beech hedge, left to itself*

Above: *Jo Down – Exmoor Artist*

The turn of the year – wassailing

Perhaps it's because Exmoor does not lie in the path of a motorway and is therefore somewhat remote from much of the country. Perhaps it's because country traditions die harder in these parts. Or perhaps it's just that people get sick to death of the mists, rain and seemingly perpetual low cloud in winter. Whatever the reason the 'wassail' or 'worsail', as Johnny tends to call it, an almighty drink up and sing along with guns, bonfires and music, is still practised on Exmoor in deepest winter when in many areas of the country it, like the horse drawn hay cart and steam threshing machine, died out long ago.

Martyn and Johnny lifting spirits in Porlock MAUREEN HARVEY

The time to witness this ancient English custom is the evening of 17th January, 'Old' Twelfth Night. The best known place is in the orchard behind the Butcher's Arms in Carhampton (and then in the pub itself) where there is an unbroken tradition of wassailing that goes back to pre-war days. The custom has been revived in recent years in Porlock, though here they manage to get through the night without a bonfire of old pallets and, just to be kind to Carhampton, the Porlock folk wassail on 'new' Twelfth Night (January 6th).

Wassail or 'all hail' means 'be of good health'. It is a fertility rite of sorts. The idea was to wake up apple trees after the depths of winter and the wassailers used both a carrot and a stick to do the job. Toast, soaked in cider and hung from the branches, was the carrot. The aim was to attract robins which would then eat the grubs and help the trees stay healthy. The stick came in the form of making a racket with old dustbin lids and gunfire, to drive out evil spirits from the orchard. Together they would help ensure a decent apple harvest in the autumn and consequently a decent amount of cider for those toiling in the fields.

In Carhampton (pronounced by the locals C'rampton) the wassail is sung by the principal, though not necessarily the oldest, villager and for many years this meant Jim Binding. Jim, alas now deceased, was only the fifth man in the village since the war to sing the wassail. Porlock's lead wassailer is Martyn Babb. Though the words are the same in both villages, Martyn's task is more onerous because he has to sing it three or four times in different orchards and he has Johnny for accompaniment.

Old apple tree we wassail thee
And hope that thou will bear
For the lord doth know where we will be
Come apples another year
To bloom well and to bear well
So happy we will be
Let every man take off his hat
And shout out to the old apple tree

Then the crowd chant the chorus.

Old apple tree we wassail thee
And hope that thou will bear
Hatfuls, capfuls, three bushel bagfuls
And a little heap under the stairs

This is followed finally by three cheers for the apple tree. Now if that does not produce a decent crop of apples, I don't know what will.

Winter into spring: Snowdrop Valley

Among the river valleys that are a lovely experience to walk at any time of year, there is one place that in the depths of winter is very special. It is part of the valley of the River Avill, below the village of Wheddon Cross.

For most of the year, walkers eager to sample the high moor's rugged delights might not give the valley more than a passing glance but for a few weeks, from mid-January, it becomes

sensationally beautiful, transformed by a carpet of snowdrops. So profuse are the flowers amid the winter vegetation that the valley floor resembles a white and green carpet.

Snowdrop Valley used to be one of Exmoor's best kept secrets but these days thousands of visitors tramp the paths and worse, clog the road to the valley with their cars and four-wheel drives. So the owners, The Badgworthy Land Company, along with the National Park and the local Cutcombe Parish Council, have come up with an ingenious solution. They close the road across the valley to traffic in February and invite visitors to take a bus from the car park at Wheddon Cross instead.

For a small fee, £3 in 2014 (with concessions for people as old as Johnny and myself), the bus will take you to where the lane crosses the river. From there you can walk a circular path through the valley and enjoy the carpet of snowdrops.

Before you get on the bus, you might appreciate a fortifying snack at the pop-up cafe in the hotel on the junction at Wheddon Cross. Rosi Davis and her partner Frank Velander open the dining room at Exmoor House as a café for just this one month early in the year and the food, all home-baked, mostly by Frank, is fantastic.

I'm partial to a toasted tea cake in the morning, Frank's homemade ones put the bought variety into some sort of perspective.

Here's the recipe he uses. It will make twelve tea cakes.

Ingredients:

200g mixed fruit
1kg strong white flour
1tsp salt
100g butter
100g sugar
500ml milk
5g yeast
1tsp sweet mixed spices

Hitching a lift to the snowdrops

Opposite: *Amongst the carpet of white and green*

Rub the butter and flour together in a large mixing bowl until they resemble fine breadcrumbs. Add the mixed spice, sugar, yeast, salt and milk. Mix together and knead. Add the mixed fruit and work it into the dough. Cover the bowl lightly with cling film, set it in a warm place and allow the dough to rise for about an hour, or until the dough has doubled in size. Then divide into 150g pieces and roll each piece into a ball. Put these on a baking tray, which you have greased and lined with baking parchment or silicon liner. Let the doughballs rise for approximately another hour, then bake at 200C for fifteen to twenty minutes.

After one of Frank's teacakes and a coffee, you'll need a walk!

While you are in the valley, as well as enjoying the amazing carpet of snowdrops, look out for the bed of a leat, a manmade waterway, and the remains of a watermill that the leat once drove.

For most of the year the archaeology in this stretch of valley is hidden under vegetation but at snowdrop time it is possible see the clues that reveal the valley's industrial past. Like so many of Exmoor's streams and rivers, the power of the water was harnessed for commercial use, for milling grain or, just as likely, for making paper.

You can carry on following the river through the woodland, turning west where the valley meets Bin Combe. The path breaks out onto open moor, with gorse and whortleberry, heading towards Dunkery Gate. From there you could take a path up to Dunkery Beacon, at 1,700 ft the highest point in Somerset, with terrific views in all directions.

Or you can catch the bus back to the village. When you get back to the car park at Wheddon Cross another culinary treat awaits. If it is lunch time, you could sample Rosi's ploughman's lunch or, if it's afternoon, her cream tea, either of which will replace the calories you worked off during the heady experience of the valley and its carpet of snowdrops.

Cream tea care of Exmoor House –
Wheddon Cross ROSI DAVIS

PART TWO
SPRING

5. Births, Marriages and (Near) Deaths
Johnny's Spring

Previous page: *Looking towards Dunkery Hill – April*

Below: *A haze of bluebells beside an Exmoor road*

IF SNOW IS THE classic image of winter on Exmoor, then bluebells are its signal that spring has arrived. Many of Exmoor's woodlands, roadsides and river valleys become a blue haze in April and May and Johnny's woodland is no different. One of his trademark shots is of badgers, who have taken up residence on his land, sniffing around the bluebells for grubs and roots.

A blaze of red campion in an Exmoor hedgerow

Badgers and bluebells –
like peaches and cream
JOHNNY KINGDOM

Spring tends to be late on Exmoor. The period from early April to the third week in May, before the tree cover is fully out, is by far the best time to see woodland plants: wild garlic, wood anemone, wild daffodils and yellow archangel as well as bluebells. Where the wood has been cleared you will find fox gloves popping up. There will be red campion, lesser celandine, wild strawberry and Welsh poppies in the hedgerows. All of Exmoor's woodlands and river valleys pay dividends for the spring walker.

Spring is a busy time for wildlife too. After the cold months of winter, the new season comes like a release for the landscape and for the animals and birds that live off it. Activity can be frenzied: birds building nests, foxes and badgers having their young, red deer stags losing their antlers, the few hares that remain on the moor boxing. And then there's Johnny. He's just as busy, scurrying around filming as much of this activity as he possibly can without driving Julie to distraction.

It was this infectious enthusiasm which wooed viewers watching his first series on television in the spring of 2000. HTV had commissioned initially just four half hour programmes but then, after surprisingly large audiences, moved quickly to a second series and the following year a third, called *A Countryman's Diary*. The programmes swept through the local TV schedule like a breath of fresh air, and HTV gathered viewers like Exmoor farmers gather hay.

A sequence shot in spring in his home village gives a clue to why the programmes were so successful. In many ways, it seemed of little consequence: a pigeon had built a nest in one of the trees on the grass verge and one day, as he was passing, Johnny noticed that a heavy, blustery rain storm had ripped the nest to pieces, depositing a chick on the ground. Most people would pass by with no more than a worried glance over their shoulder but not Johnny. Here was a wildlife problem that needed a solution and he could provide it. He went back to his house and collected some old chicken wire. Returning, he climbed the tree, rebuilt the nest and put the chick back in its home. Job done – or so he thought.

Unfortunately, his nest-building skills were not much better than the mother pigeon's and, after another fierce storm, the nest fell apart for a second time. But Johnny is a persistent soul. Undeterred, he rebuilt the nest yet again, reuniting the chick with its mother once more. This time, like a father watching his toddler through the school fence, he kept a watchful eye on both. A few days later the young pigeon had fledged and flown. No big deal but a life saved.

Doing all that merely to save the life of one pigeon chick, spotting the problem, having the empathy and the confidence to try and solve it and then persisting until he finally got it right would be beyond most people but not beyond Johnny.

However, there's a twist to the story that illustrates the uniqueness of Johnny's appeal. Not only did he twice rebuild the nest and save the life of the pigeon, he filmed it all on his video camera, alone, without any professional assistance. The results were brilliant. A professional cameraman would have considered Johnny's pictures terrible: it was pouring with rain as he filmed himself, so there was water on the lens; he put the camera on a tripod and shot from only one angle; and the sound quality was dire. But who cared? Certainly not the audience, jaded by their usual TV diet of perfectly shot but often totally faked natural history filming. They lapped up Johnny's sequence because it was a successful wildlife rescue with the ring of truth.

In fact, most of Johnny's filming was 'rough at the edges' and, as he became more proficient, he attempted to improve the quality of his shots. Paradoxically, that took away some of the authenticity of the material. As one commissioning editor said to me: 'If I want blue chip wildlife filming, I can get it in bucketfuls from the BBC Natural History Unit. What I want from these programmes is Johnny being Johnny. There's no one else like him on television.'

That Johnny likes a challenge is nothing new but snakes, especially adders have always been a particular issue for him. The trouble is that he doesn't like adders. He's not alone; there are plenty of people out there who feel the same. Perhaps it's because snakes don't have any cuddly bits that we usually associate with wildlife: no legs, no fur, no ears. Or perhaps it's their reputation. A bite from an adder rarely kills a human but it can be really painful and will need medical attention straight away.

Adders are common on Exmoor. They come out of hibernation in the spring and lurk in the banks and hedgerows, especially where there is a combination of dead bracken and a warm, sunny aspect. You don't have to stray from a path to see an adder but you must be quiet. If they hear or feel you coming they are much more likely to slither off and hide in the undergrowth than take a bite. They are easy to recognize: the male is grey with a distinct zigzag pattern along the length of his back, the female larger and often a reddish-brown colour, but with a similar zigzag stripe.

Adders are active through the spring and summer and their first task after a winter of not doing much, apart from sleeping, is to mate. Well, not quite the first; if only life was that simple. No, the first job for the males is to establish their superiority among their fellows. Which will be the alpha male adder? They find out through a display of wrestling and dancing and the routine can be spectacular. Johnny filmed it in the spring of 2014. When two males go head to head they will often not only twist and entwine with each other but raise almost their whole body from the ground, looking as if they are indeed dancing. As always after these testosterone-driven routines there will be a winner whose prize is to mate with the waiting female, while the loser slinks off as fast as he can.

Oh what a tangled web we weave – adders mating
JOHNNY KINGDOM

After one session filming dancing snakes in spring 2014, Johnny made an equally quick getaway to his land and not just to escape the adder. He was desperate to find out whether his big winter Grand Design, the badger house, had paid dividends.

During the early months of 2014, Johnny and his mate Bob Sampson had been up to their knees in squelchy red Devon clay, digging a massive hole, installing Bob's old septic tank as the badger home, laying drainage pipes that would act as runs and generally getting in a mess.

An underground badger house, wired for filming, was the latest in Johnny's ploys to film his favourite mammal. Over the years he's moved on from lying in the bracken filming badgers in their wild habitat to building comfortable hides close to setts. He's erected obstacle courses, constructed wheels a badger can turn to get a shower of peanuts and experimented with filming underground using a mobile camera attached to a miniature vehicle with a passing resemblance to a moon buggy.

But the badger house was on a grander scale altogether. Johnny had never before attempted anything so ambitious.

The build was finished by the end of January and now, in the spring, he was hoping against hope he would get tenants for his new badger home. There was no rent to pay, the house was part-furnished with hay brought in by him and there was the additional inducement of a free meal every so often. It was the sort of pad that might suit most students. But when it comes to house lets, badgers are probably more particular than students. More often than not they have perfectly adequate underground homes that they have themselves built. They cannot point the finger at someone else's dodgy workmanship and plumbing, the building work is all their own. Moreover, in their own homes they know where they are. And their setts are complicated affairs.

The badger house – Johnny's Grand Design

At home in the new house
JOHNNY KINGDOM

A mature badger sett, of the sort found on Johnny's land, might have five or six different entrances. Badgers are communal animals so a number of families might live in one large sett. There will be various chambers, some for sleeping, some for feeding, others for giving birth; but no indoor toilets. Badgers, notoriously clean animals, have outside loos. It's one of the ways you can identify a badger sett, you might see badger droppings outside it. Another telltale sign is the bedding that they have dragged outside the sett to dry out or freshen up. A final clue is the hairs you might find in the bedding or on the ground: quite thin, black or grey with a white tip at one end.

Would any badger take up Johnny's kind offer? He was about to find out.

He kept a watchful eye on other setts that badgers had built, in front of which he had positioned cameras. He was looking for any clues that badgers were on the move after the long winter. Johnny is too experienced to expect results immediately, he knew he would have to wait. A couple of weeks went by, during which time nothing happened. Then, at last, he was reviewing overnight film from one of the cameras and saw a lot of activity.

This was the moment of truth. Although badgers from 'natural' setts were starting to move about, would they use the one he'd built?

One night in April he took Bob into the box that acts as his studio. All the wires from the cameras in the badger house lead there and it's the hub of the filming, his very own Springwatch control room.

Bob was certainly impressed as he cast his eye over Johnny's and Rupert's handiwork. As well as being the cameraman for most of his recent programmes on television, Rupert is responsible for making work much of the electronic gadgetry dotted around Johnny's land. Johnny and Bob sat quietly as he flicked switches, turned on cameras and generally made himself comfortable.

Then, to their unbridled delight, they saw badgers in the badger house. It was hard to tell who was having more fun, the badgers or the two men watching. They all behaved like kids. The badgers were tumbling around the sett as playfully as the two grown men were jigging around Johnny's studio. They counted five badgers in the sett and were able to flick between cameras to get as much enjoyment from the activity as did the badgers themselves. Johnny's Grand Design had worked.

Johnny is lucky because his own land enables him to watch badgers day and night. Not everyone is so fortunate. But if like most of us, you don't happen to have badgers on your doorstep, it doesn't mean you can't get pleasure from watching them. You just need a bit of field craft to find them in the wild. Here are some of Johnny's tips for badger watching.

First of all, find your sett. Badgers like to dig and they are very good at it, with ferociously powerful front claws, like miniature black and white versions of the earth-moving equipment you see wherever a road is being built or the foundations of a building excavated. Their setts can be quite small, with just a few holes, or huge rambling constructions that stretch across a wide area. They are most commonly found in deciduous or broad leafed woodland; however you can also find them in hedgerows, on the slopes of open fields and in the steep banks of some lanes. A clue can be the proximity of elder trees because badgers like elder berries. They pass the berries through their faeces outside the sett, the berries take root and, hey presto, elder bushes sprout.

Once you've found a sett, visit it a couple of times during the day to get to know the area. Second, check that you will be allowed to watch badgers there. Some landowners, as Johnny has found to his cost, can be prickly when it comes to allowing people on their land. And third, don't get shot by one of the men hired to cull badgers by DEFRA, the Department for Food, Environment and Rural Affairs. The area in which Johnny lives is one of the parts of the country where there is a controlled cull of badgers in an ongoing experiment to eliminate TB in cattle.

Fourthly, watch out where you put your feet. Some badger setts have concealed back doors you might not notice as you wander round the field. Filming badgers, a television colleague of mine gave her crew the obligatory health and safety briefing about this, only to see the cameraman almost immediately put his foot down just such a hole and nearly break a leg.

Spring is the best time of the year to watch badgers. The young are born in February and by the end of March they will be coming above ground. Late April to early May, while evenings are getting lighter and the leaf cover is not yet out, is a good time to see what is going on. Johnny has shown time and time again that it is a myth that badgers emerge from the sett only at night. He's filmed them many times during daylight, though late afternoon into dusk is the best time.

Get there early. Don't wait for the badgers to be out of the sett because then they will hear you approach and your chances of seeing anything are gone. Just as important, make sure they cannot smell you. Badgers have a fantastic sense of smell so it is best not to arrive doused in perfume or aftershave; leave the Lynx at home. The way you approach the sett is crucial: make sure the wind is blowing from the sett towards you. If the wind is behind you, blowing toward the sett, badgers will pick up your scent straight away and will stay tucked up in their beds for the night. They won't be able to distinguish you from one of the Ministry's contracted shooters so they will play safe and stay out of the way.

If you can ensure the badger cannot hear or smell you, you're more than half way to a successful evening badger watching. Badgers don't have good eyesight but nevertheless it's a good idea to wear dark clothes. Johnny wears full camouflage when he's out stalking (actually, he wears pretty much full camouflage even when he's not out stalking). Warm clothes and gloves are a good idea, gleaming watches and jewellery a bad one. If you have a pair of field glasses you can keep a good distance, perhaps behind a tree and enjoy an extremely pleasant couple of hours observing badgers just as Johnny does, perfect.

A woodland badger sett – one of its many entrances

A badger and her four cubs
JOHNNY KINGDOM

6. Animals

A hare – with an all round view
JOHNNY KINGDOM

Opposite: *A young hare – a leveret*
RUPERT SMITH

AS ANY ESTATE agent will tell you, the key to the property market is 'location, location, location.' For Johnny Kingdom, watching wildlife, it's 'patience, patience, patience.'

'You won't get nowhere if you don't have patience,' he often says. A man who is impetuous in almost all other areas, when it comes to wildlife, Johnny has patience in spades. In the spring, when animals are busy rearing their young, it has paid off handsomely in three very different situations. One was while filming hares, a second filming foxes and a third when he was in pursuit of one of Exmoor's newer residents, wild boar. Taken together, the three scenarios show just how good Johnny's field craft is and how patience invariably pays dividends.

Brown hares

Brown hares are not common in the West Country. They prefer open spaces, grasslands and large fields of the sort found on the Wiltshire Downs or in the arable areas of Eastern England. But if you know where to look, or you know someone who knows where to look, then you can find them on Exmoor and Johnny usually does know someone who knows where to look.

On this particular occasion it was a friend, Graham Clemence, who farms at Kings Nympton. As so often happens when Johnny's filming wildlife, he might go to a place to see one species and end up filming something altogether unexpected.

It was late March and Johnny was hoping to film a barn owl Graham had told him about. He'd hidden himself behind some bushes with a view of the barn where he thought the owl might be. He waited, and waited, then waited some more. He never did see the owl, which is not unusual; wildlife expeditions often end in failure but that only adds to the adrenalin rush when they turn out to be successful. While Johnny was waiting for the owl to make an appearance he was surprised by a hare that popped out in front of him, galumphing along the path past the barn to disappear into the field behind. The brief sighting gave Johnny an idea.

A couple of days went by before he could get back to the farm with our cameraman. They behaved just like boys who'd been given the key to the sweet shop. Graham told them in which field he'd last spotted the hare and told them to be careful of the cows. In something of a hurry, the two of them forgot about the cows and set off in search of hares, hoping at this time of year they might see 'boxing'.

Witnessing two hares 'boxing' is a special wildlife moment. The hares will race around the field, tumbling over each other and then standing on their hind legs as if throwing punches. Many people assume that boxing hares are two males but that is not the case. It is more often than not a female fighting off a male. He might be ready to mate but she is not. It's another of those wildlife courtship rituals.

To get a shot of this courtship activity requires a lot of patience and not a little skill with the camera. The brown hare is the fastest mammal in Britain and it can run at speeds of up to 35 or 45 miles per hour (depending on which internet site you reference). The 'turn' is astonishing: the hare will leap high into the air, ten or even 15 feet, and turn 180 degrees as it does so. This speed and turn are the hare's only defences in the face of a pursing predator.

Johnny and the cameraman made their way to the field where the hare had last been sighted. Followed at an appropriate distance by the cameraman, he scanned the field and saw the cows grazing in one corner. Unconcerned, he looked for signs of the hare, perhaps a couple of ears pointing skywards.

Hares don't rely on escaping underground for protection from predators, as rabbits do but on speed and alertness. Their eyes are positioned to the side of the head so they have excellent all round vision, not to mention an acute sense of smell and a huge pair of rear legs that power a slender body, giving the animal its speed. If you watch a running hare with its graceful bounding stride you can see where the expression 'to hare about' came from.

Their only living quarters is a flattened piece of grassland known as a form. This is where the female gives birth and rears her leverets. These are born with their eyes open and after only five days they can outrun a fox. But those first five days are crucial because they are very vulnerable when first born. While modern agricultural techniques and shooting have reduced the population of hares, foxes are their main natural predator. A fox will often move systematically through a field looking for newborn leverets and take them at will.

Johnny had not been long in the field before he saw a single hare lying low, about 200 yards distant. He got down on his stomach and crawled across the meadow on all fours, keeping a thistle between him and the hare to stay out of view of his quarry. The cameraman caught the view of his backside wiggling along. Though it looked odd, it's the only way to keep out of sight when there is little cover. The hare remained totally still, it had not seen him; so far, so good. Johnny began to film and the cameraman, a few yards back, filmed Johnny. After some time in that position he decided he wanted a closer view. He would have to move and there was little chance the hare wouldn't notice him. So it proved. As he crawled forward, the hare lifted itself up to take a look. Johnny got a terrific shot, then the hare bolted.

Both men were pleased: they hadn't got boxing hares but they had some lovely pictures. They'd been in the field for about an hour and stood up to make their way back to the farm. Then all hell broke loose, in the shape of a thoroughly cheesed-off bull. It had been with the cows in the field and saw Johnny as a trespasser. It approached in the way angry bulls do, snorting with head bowed low and swaying from side to side, feet scrubbing the ground, a sight with which no one ever wants to be confronted.

What to do? Make a run for it? That is the very worst thing, running would have only encouraged the bull. It was now that another side of Johnny came to the fore: his calmness under pressure, his ability to think through a dangerous life-threatening situation. And, of course, his patience.

His response was to do nothing, just sit tight and make no sudden moves that might further antagonise the bull. It worked. Gradually the bull calmed down and backed away and after a while Johnny and his cameraman were able to creep towards the gate. Outwardly they were calm, inwardly they were anything but. The evidence is on the video the cameraman shot. Astonishingly, he'd had the presence of mind to continue filming as Johnny explained quietly how they could get out of the mess they were in. Johnny often talks to animals and on this occasion he talked to the bull. 'Let the bull get to know us,' he whispered to the cameraman, and then addressed the bull: 'Don't worry, we're not going after your ladies, I've got my own at home.'

The whole scene lasted only a few minutes but at the time it must have seemed an eternity. It certainly did to Johnny.

A vixen at home with her young
RUPERT SMITH

Foxes

When it came to finding and filming foxes, it took patience of a wholly different kind.

There are more foxes in Britain than there have ever been. Estimates (and be careful about which website you look at) put the number at just under 300,000. Yet the only time most of us see a fox in the countryside is when it is flattened on the road or, if we live in a town, sniffing round a waste bin or strolling through the garden as if it owned it.

In country areas spotting foxes is much more difficult because a rural fox needs a much bigger territory than an urban fox. There is more cover and they are brilliant at staying out of the way. A fox will see and smell you long before you see and smell it. So if you're interested in watching foxes, it's helpful to know something about how and where they live and their behaviour patterns.

Foxes are the perfectly adapted predator. They can live on open moorland, in dense woodland, by the coast or under your conservatory. They have a varied diet. Johnny has in the past filmed foxes behind a house where they were attracted by the owner feeding them dogfood sandwiches, on wholemeal bread, of course. In the wild, they eat anything from blackberries to earthworms, from small rodents to chickens and pheasants. And what they don't eat immediately they will bury for later.

Like hares, foxes live above ground, though unlike hares, they have their cubs below ground. They are much less particular about their home than are badgers. A fox's den will often be more rough and ready than a badger sett. In fact, foxes are good squatters and will sometimes occupy an

Tony Thorne – a good friend to Johnny

Let me entertain you – Johnny building a run for his badgers
JOHNNY KINGDOM

old badger sett. Johnny has known them even share a sett with a family of badgers, though they did have separate entrances.

Cubs are born in February. They spend the first four or five weeks underground, coming up to the surface around April. A good time to try to spot foxes is when the cubs first emerge from their den. One of Johnny's tactics is to find a den and then keep watching it, day after day. But even the best laid plans can be rendered irrelevant by the odd stroke of good fortune. One of his most memorable sightings of cubs emerging from their underground home once again revolved around the good nature of a friend.

Tony Thorne, now deceased, sad to say, farmed alone in the hamlet of Twitchen, a place so small a car driver might pass through without even noticing. There are just a few houses packed together snugly, like peas in a pod and a couple of farms, one owned by Tony's sister, Mary.

Tony was a remarkable farmer with an extraordinary farm. His family came from the hamlet and he had spent his whole life there. A hospitable man, he always had a tot of whisky on hand for a visitor. He'd suffered a bad accident, losing an eye when the blade of a circular saw he was using shattered. He knew he had been lucky: that saw could have cost him his life.

In the autumn of 2001, Johnny suddenly and inexplicably faced a problem. For years, he had been filming badgers from an elaborate hide he'd erected on land where he'd been given permission to film by its owners, Terry and Carol Rudd.

Then access to the hide, across a separate piece of land owned by someone else, was suddenly denied. When Johnny told Tony how devastated he was, the farmer came up with a simple solution that saved the day. He would let Johnny build a new hide on some of his land, overlooking a badger sett on the edge of woodland.

Johnny was grateful. On a bitterly cold Boxing Day he organised a gang of mates to put up scaffolding for the new hide. Working off too much Christmas pudding appealed to them and they laboured hard all morning, only to find they'd erected the structure upside down. Maybe there was too much brandy in the pudding. They spent the afternoon rebuilding.

The rickety but effective hide was soon up and running. With video cameras focusing on the badger sett Johnny waited patiently for badger cubs to pop their heads above ground. Imagine his surprise then, when one April morning he turned up bright and early and switched on his cameras only to find, after waiting for half an hour, not a badger cub but a fox cub.

Here was a golden opportunity for a sequence in the programmes we were making at the time. The following day, a crew set off before dawn from Bristol to join him at Twitchen. The sun was just rising as they made their way across Tony's fields and positioned themselves in the hide. They waited and waited while they got colder and colder but no fox cub showed up. By lunch time they had had enough and trudged discontentedly back across the fields.

'Shame, but we'll just have to come back tomorrow,' was Johnny's reaction. We couldn't but he did and once again his old adage about patience paid off. He was in position at sunrise and as he

A single fox cub waits for his siblings…
JOHNNY KINGDOM

…to come out to play
JOHNNY KINGDOM

*What we did on our holiday –
Johnny's Boxing Day hide on
Tony's land*

One that got away – an Exmoor wild boar JOHNNY KINGDOM

It worked yesterday – Johnny rigging a remote camera

switched on the camera, there in front of him was the fox cub, poking its pointed nose and bright eyes out of the badger sett. Then it was out, frolicking on the hillside, to be followed by another and another and yet another cub. In all, Johnny counted five fox cubs tumbling around and rolling around in the grass. He may even have said: 'What do you want prettier than that?'

'Wild' boar

There are many examples of activists who, concerned about the welfare of captured 'wild' animals, release them into the freedom of the British countryside. The story of mink being helped out of British fur farms and then going on to terrorise the vole population is just one of many.

In January 2006 Exmoor had its own 'animal rights release' saga when someone broke open the fences of Woodland Wild Boar farm near West Anstey. About a hundred boars, young and old, male and female, made a dash for freedom. The owner, Alan Dedames, had brought over the wild boar from France. In media interviews he reckoned that most of the females were pregnant but the boars, even those with large hairy tusks, would not attack unless cornered.

All hell broke loose. The aftermath resembled a Wild West shootout. Farmers, members of the hunt, many carrying shotguns or rifles, an array of spectators and others hoping to grab some of the action, and some of the pork, turned out. They hoped to recover as many as possible of the animals that had escaped. Unsurprisingly, with the sound of quad bikes, Land Rovers and over-excited hunters filling the air, they were not particularly successful.

About thirty boar were recaptured and a small number shot. The rest got away. Wild boar are good at concealing themselves and the Yeo Valley area is now home to a small population of these creatures, living mostly in woodland, turning up earth and rooting for food. They are particularly attracted to the bed of the defunct Taunton to Barnstaple railway line and the wasteland that surrounds it. They are partial to food that gamekeepers put out for pheasants, tipping over the drums to gorge themselves. The pheasant shoot on the Molland Estate has been a relatively easy target for them; there are so many birds it provides a glut of fodder.

None of this bothered Johnny. He was hoping that some of the newly-emancipated boar would find sanctuary on his land and was as keen as the next man to shoot a few – with a video camera, rather than a shotgun.

He first realised he had attracted some of these visitors when he saw the effect of their foraging on ground close to his pond. It looked as if someone had been turning it over with a garden fork. Thrilled to bits after finding the site, he tracked their movements across the land. Like many wild animals wild boar are most active at night so if Johnny was going to film them he reasoned he would have to be out for long periods after dusk.

He set up a couple of cameras overlooking a route he thought they might take, as well as the feeding site he'd found, running cables back a hundred yards or so to a makeshift hide. Then he returned in the early evening to wait. Nothing happened. He saw deer and heard an owl but no wild boar. Disappointed, he went home vowing to return the following evening. Again nothing happened and nothing on the third or fourth night. Should he give up?

No way: this is Johnny Kingdom I am talking about. With every setback he became more determined. It took no less than eight evening visits before he finally saw what he'd been looking for. A wild boar, with tusks showing clearly and followed by its family, stepped gingerly into the area he was filming. They seemed nervous, suspicious of any alien sound or movement but in the hide Johnny was well away from them and filmed with impunity.

He was elated. It had taken more than a week but, unlike the hunters brandishing guns and chasing around on quad bikes, he'd managed to shoot the wild boars of Exmoor.

Free at last – a wild boar family on Johnny and Julie's land
JOHNNY KINGDOM

7. The Moor in Spring

SPRING FLOWERS, plenty of wildlife and fantastic views: exploring Exmoor's coast in the spring reaps terrific rewards.

Woody Bay to Heddon's Mouth (and back)

What better way to enjoy the coast than by walking the stretch from Woody Bay to Heddon's Mouth, an 8-mile round trip, an absolute treat for the wildlife enthusiast. It's a walk that's full of variety and mid-June is the perfect time to take in its breath-taking beauty. With one of Exmoor's pubs at the halfway stage and a delicious cream tea in a delightful tea garden to look forward to, there's also plenty of opportunity for a refreshing break.

The walk begins in the car park above the appropriately named Woody Bay. Head up the hill on the road to the first hairpin bend, then follow the path signposted Hunter's Inn into woodland. To call it a path does the route scant justice. According to Harriet Bridle, author of *Woody Bay* (Reading, 1991), it was constructed as a carriageway in 1893-95 by one of the large landowners in the area, Colonel Benjamin Greene Lake. His idea was to transport gentlefolk from the villas around the bay by carriage to his hostelry, Hunter's Inn. It's impossible to be certain how many Victorian ladies in their finery would have made the trip but what I do know is that Lake managed to create one of the finest walks in England.

The woodland on the first mile or so feels completely natural though it is anything but. The sessile oak trees were to Victorian tanners what fields of waving wheat were to thatchers: a carefully managed crop. The oak was grown not so much for timber but for its bark, which was stripped from the trunk and used in tanning workshops to cure hides. Look closely and you will see that most of the trees sprout from the base, like the leaves of daffodils. Woodsmen cut back the trees just above ground level, a technique of woodland management known as coppicing. Coppicing prevented the trees from growing too tall and instead encouraged a flourish of thinner stems from the base, providing more wood and more bark for the leather industry. The wood itself would have been made into hurdles for fencing or burned for charcoal.

All that is now gone. For more than a century, nature has been allowed to re-colonise this part of the world and it's worth stopping from time to time to appreciate the wildlife that is part of the re-colonisation. From May to late June you might see a host of woodland birds busy building nests

The start of the carriage way to Hunter's Inn

Woody Bay and behind it Lee Bay and the Valley of Rocks

A large skipper in a glade

Top: *A wren takes a breather in woodland cover* JOHNNY KINGDOM

Above: *A male stonechat resting on a branch of gorse* JOHNNY KINGDOM

or feeding their young. The area is popular with tree creepers and nuthatches as well as wrens, robins and woodpeckers.

All along the path there are breaks in the woodland canopy where wild rose and blackberry flourish alongside bracken and whortleberry. Stop at any of these on a warm morning and there will be butterflies. The path is crossed by steep 'racks', routes taken by red deer from the shelter of the woodland to the pasture above it.

After about a mile and a half of woodland the path suddenly opens out, edged by gorse, bracken and heather, to reveal incredible views. The outline of the hog's back cliffs in front are matched by the panoramas across the water to the South Wales coast. You might see walkers on the lower path, which you will be taking on the return trip. Like Johnny, you might spot and photograph a stonechat taking a breather on a prominent gorse bush, or a skylark soaring upwards.

Further along the path a sign points to 'Martinhoe only'. It's worth taking the short diversion. It opens out onto an earthwork called Martinhoe Fort, one the few sites of Roman occupation on

Exmoor. It's a spectacular setting: the views are better here than anywhere else on the walk and it's easy to appreciate why the Romans chose this spot to keep a lookout for marauders from across the water, the Silurian tribes of Wales, who were their bitter enemies.

A mile or so on from these views, at Highveer Point, the carriageway turns, dropping down through more sessile oak woodland with wild honeysuckle in the undergrowth, a sign that dormice might be nesting here; they use honeysuckle to line their nests. Onwards through a gate you reach Hunter's Inn and a little further up the valley, a National Trust Shop.

Don't be fooled into imagining that the shop will provide an alternative to the fare dished up at this Swiss chalet-style hotel. Put out of your mind luscious National Trust scones, clotted cream and jam, lemon drizzle and chocolate cake. If you don't you will be disappointed. Sadly, a covenant prevents the Trust from selling food here. The location of the Hunter's Inn is delightful, with tables outside that catch the morning and lunchtime sun.

After a suitable time spent feasting at the pub or picnicking by the river you might feel inclined to head straight back to Woody Bay along the lower coastal path. It is worth resisting the

Top: *Hunter's Inn today*

Above: *Hunter's Inn as it used to be – before fire destroyed the thatch* HARRIET BRIDLE

Left: *Looking west towards Trentishoe and Holdstone Downs – part of Exmoor's majestic coastline*

Top: *A small tortoiseshell feeds on the thistles in the meadows towards Heddon's Mouth*

Above: *Sea campion – so many flowers it's like a rock garden*

urge. Do as Johnny does, take a detour to Heddon's Mouth. Follow the road on the south side of the inn until it bends to the right. There's a good sized track with a five bar gate and stile leading to Heddon's Mouth with woodland on the left and exceptionally interesting meadows to the right, owned by the National Trust. They remind me of what England used to be like when I was young because they have been allowed to revert to a time before farmers sprayed pesticides and insecticides that killed wild flowers and insects and the birds which relied on them.

Take a look at the thistles in the marshy parts of the meadow. Varieties of butterflies love them. You'll find more feeding on buddleia in the hedgerow. It's a wonderful sight and this area is one of the best places in the whole of Exmoor to see them.

Carry on down to the coast. The terrain here is like walking through a massive rock garden. Loose scree, tumbled down the steep-sided valley by centuries of water, ice and wind erosion, drenched in sun in the late spring, provides perfect conditions for kidney vetch, thrift and rock stonecrop.

The stream – for the River Heddon is hardly more than that – follows this serene valley until it reaches the sea. You might curse yourself for eating your picnic earlier because this is surely the

Heddon's Mouth – just the place for that picnic

perfect place to indulge yourself. You could munch your sandwiches on the pebble beach, on the banks of the stream while dangling your feet in the clear cold water, or on one of the benches, provided by the Trust that overlook a lime kiln at the mouth of the river.

The lime kiln is a reminder that this area was at one time so much more than merely a magnet for walkers and tourists. The path was the route taken by teams of packhorses, laden with lime, bound for Exmoor's fields. The acid, peat-based soils on the hills were sweetened with lime from many local kilns, the ruins of which are spread along the coast like beacons. Indeed, when they were active, only a century ago, they would have blazed like beacons. Boats landed limestone on the beach to be burned in the kiln with a mix of charcoal, wood and bracken.

Before you go look up towards the cliffs on either side of the valley. You might spot peregrine falcons which nest on these cliffs. Johnny spent days here a few years ago just to get a photograph of one.

The return journey follows the path for a couple of hundred yards until a wooden bridge crosses the stream. Cross the bridge and head upstream until you meet the lower coastal path that takes you back to Woody Bay.

As you climb out of Heddon's Mouth you are in for yet another cocktail of glorious views. But you need to be careful. It's best here not to walk and try to spot wildlife at the same time. The path narrows, becoming too risky for multitasking and men are not much good at multitasking at the best of times.

Once the climb is done the path turns east at Highveer Point and the walking gets easier, though the steep drop to the left demands you should keep looking where you are going. After about a mile there are more splendid views of hog's back cliffs tumbling down to the sea, as well as a feature in the cliffs, a rock with a hole through it. It seems impossible that the sea could have created this natural wonder known as Wringapeak. The place is lovely at any time of the year but the highlight for those interested in Exmoor's birds occurs in late spring with a glimpse of the colonies of razorbills and guillemots that nest on the Peak and the surrounding cliffs. Spring is the only time these birds come close to the coast. They spend the rest of the year at sea so it makes the walk in May or June all the more worthwhile.

A male peregrine waits on the rocks above Heddon's Mouth
JOHNNY KINGDOM

A group of guillemots takes a break from fishing PETER HILTON

Wringapeak home to colonies of sea birds

Above: *The curse of the National Trust – rhododendron*

Above right: *So that's why it's called Woody Bay*

After Wringapeak you are not far from the end of the walk. Pass beside a waterfall, a lovely surprise, and then you are back in the sessile oak plantation. Walking through the woodland you will come across numbers of rhododendron bushes looking so exquisite at this time of the year that it is difficult to appreciate that the plant is a problem for the National Trust, who own this land. Rhododendron is an environmental disaster. It overwhelms the ground on which it grows, leaving it like a desert. Nothing will grow under its canopy and it is so difficult to eradicate that it has become a real headache for the Trust.

One more mile of woodland brings you to the road. There is a relatively steep walk back to the car park or, if you turn left, an equally steep stroll down to the beach at Woody Bay. It's well worth the detour before going home.

Steps down to the beach take you to a place that, again looks completely natural but on closer inspection reveals that people have endeavoured to make money out of this bay. There is the inevitable lime kiln, built in 1753, with a slipway down to the beach for hauling quantities of limestone and coal from Wales. But Woody Bay was exploited for another commercial purpose.

There was an effort in the late nineteenth century to attract day trippers and holiday makers. It was part of a grand plan by Colonel Lake, the man who had the carriageway built. He saw the potential for Woody Bay to become another Lynton, a holiday Mecca for the Victorians. He built a sea-water swimming pool with a changing hut for ladies. His problem was how to get people to the bay. Not every woman in her Victorian finery wanted to risk the bumpy carriageway and the uneven steps, taking her past what would have been in those days a dirty, working lime kiln, to bathe on a rocky beach.

The Colonel came up with an ingenious solution. He would bring them to the bay by sea, on a paddle-steamer. To land his visitors, he decided to build a pier, an enormous structure that could cope with the vicissitudes of the changing tides. Work began in 1895 and the first steamer brought intrepid holidaymakers to the bay two years later. A man after my own heart, Colonel Lake had even built a welcoming tearoom on the pier. A clergyman from the parish of Martinhoe, the Reverend R.W. Oldham, an enthusiastic amateur photographer in the days when rural clergymen had time for hobbies like photographic printing, captured it for posterity. Sadly for Colonel Lake's bank balance, the structure lasted only a few years. In 1899 and 1900, violent storms got the better of it and it became another heroic Exmoor failure.

Coming up the hill to the car park from the beach you could turn left and walk (or drive, if your feet forbid more walking) a mile and half to a Victorian gothic house called Lee Abbey, where you will be rewarded with a perfectly located tea garden. The house dates from the 1850s, becoming a Christian community only after 1945. The garden is run by volunteers, mostly in their twenties and thirties, who live for a time at the abbey.

With tables dotted about in all sorts of nooks and crannies, the garden is just what the walker needs after a day on the coastal path. Light lunches and delicious homemade cakes and scones are

Above left: *The pier in 1899*
MRS J. OLDHAM ARCHIVE

Above right: *The pier, or what's left of it, today*

Below: *One of the many gorgeous cakes at Lee Abbey tea garden*

dished up from a counter. It's sometimes said – well, said by me, anyway – that a really good café needs only three varieties of cake: something with chocolate, a Victoria sponge and a fruitcake. More than that and you are spoiled for choice. The tea garden at Lee Abbey has them all, as well as homemade scones cooling on a rack. What more could one ask for? Take a seat in the garden and enjoy.

While you are in the area you would be well advised to go the extra mile (well, a couple) and look at the old goats in the wonderfully atmospheric landscape called Valley of Rocks. And I don't mean Johnny and his cameraman, they will be filming them. The feral goats have grazed the hills and steep slopes to the sea for as long as anyone can remember and like every other animal that eats anything on Exmoor many see them as an asset. They keep down the scrub, stop small trees growing on the cliffs and generally look good for visitors. What's not to like about them?

Bracken, it's delicious – a feral goat in the Valley of Rocks

PART THREE
SUMMER

8. Fêtes Accomplished
Johnny's Summer

Johnny making hay while the sun shines

Previous page: *Porlock Common and beyond, Porlock Bay in August – the best time to enjoy the heather moors*

LIKE THE REST of the year summer for Johnny is busy, crammed with appointments with wildlife on his land and, on the moor, engagements of a different kind.

Summer is the time when he hopes to reap the rewards from all the hours of work he puts in on his land through winter and spring. His cameras are in place, nesting boxes cleaned and food available for visiting wildlife. He'll be hoping to catch a wild boar or two with his night vision

Harvest the old-fashioned way
MARY WERNER

cameras; birds, blue tits or woodpeckers, nesting in one of the fifty or so boxes and activity on the pond. If he's lucky he might see nesting ducks or geese. If he's unlucky it will be a heron taking his fish. There are always dragonflies hovering and butterflies in the meadow above the pond.

Johnny has around 20 acres of grass which, in June, he cuts for hay. It's a sight you don't see very often these days. So many farmers now produce silage that the sight of grass lying on the ground, drying in the midsummer sun, is rare. Even rarer is the way the same patch of land looked a few years ago when he grew wheat.

Most varieties of wheat grown in England these days are short-stemmed but Johnny went for a taller, old-fashioned strain. The wheat, waving gently in the summer breeze, looked terrific – and so did the deer that came into the field to nip off quite a lot of the heads. Undeterred, Johnny pressed on and harvested the crop in traditional fashion, with a reaper binder. It's the sort of machine that was a common sight on British wheat fields until technology wiped it out and replaced it with the infinitely less romantic, if super-efficient, combine harvester.

What is so appealing about the reaper binder is that you can see the process in action, whereas with combine harvesting it's all hidden inside the machine. The reaper binder cuts the wheat, binds it then spits it out onto the ground in small bundles. The bundles are then stacked or 'stooked' by hand to dry out in the sun. It is a classic rural British scene that would not look out of place in a Constable painting or a Thomas Hardy novel.

The dry stooks are taken back to a barn where the heads are separated from the stalks. While the wheat is milled for flour or fed to livestock, the straw is stored for use, as likely as not by a thatcher. Thatchers like the long-straw wheat that Johnny grew because new, short-stemmed varieties are of no use to them. As long-straw wheat has become less common, thatching with straw has been slowly dying out, water reed taking its place.

Johnny's wheat was used by a thatcher friend to restore the thatch on a North Devon farm house. It's an initiative applauded by environment agencies and conservationists, who want to see thatched buildings in Devon restored with traditional local materials rather than imported ones, even if some of the imports are coming only from the other side of England.

Away from his land, Johnny will be looking for newborn red deer calves. June is the optimum time for them and for the much rarer (for Exmoor) roe deer. Summer is the time when roe deer mate and Johnny will take excursions east to the Brendon Hills to try to catch the rut. Not as spectacular as the red deer rut – roe buck antlers are considerably smaller than those of red deer stags – Johnny is nevertheless compelled towards it.

Roe deer are found throughout England and Wales, though they are not as common on Exmoor as red deer. They live in individual family groups rather than herds and they are smaller too. The buck stands at about 3 to 4 feet and the doe 2 to 3 feet. Kids are born in May or June.

Their natural habitat is woodland surrounded by pasture, ideally fields of tall grasses. There are lots of them on the Somerset Levels and Johnny will often go there to see them. They love the

A summer visitor to the land – a roe deer buck JOHNNY KINGDOM

willow, or withy, beds and drive farmers to distraction by nibbling the new growth. One of their most attractive features, which Johnny has caught on camera many times, is their movement across the ground. As they race across the landscape, leaping high into the air, they remind you of small herds of impala or gazelle on the African savannah. So beautifully rhythmic is their stride, it's as if they are bounding across a series of children's bouncy castles or trampolines.

But at this time of year Johnny is also likely to be involved in some of Exmoor's summer village shows. The big one is Dunster Show in August. Exford holds the Devon and Somerset Staghounds puppy show in July, but Brayford gets in early: their fête, with a duck race as the star event, is held towards the end of May.

Brayford is a special place for Johnny. He was born close to the village, went to junior school there and, when he left school, he worked in the local quarry. His mother lived there all her life and she and other members of his family are buried in the graveyard. It was beneath the shadow of the tower of the 800-year-old High Bray church that Johnny dug his first grave, with his father, at only twelve years of age.

So you can imagine his pleasure when he was asked to come back and open the day's proceedings. No animals were harmed during the race: the thousand ducks launched into the river were all plastic.

Alongside the duck race, there was a dog show in which Johnny and Julie's dog won a second prize – no nepotism there, I hope. There were cream teas, a plant stall, cake stall, bring and buy, all you would expect from a village fête. And although it poured with rain in the morning, by the time everything got underway at 2pm, the sun was shining.

The Brayford duck race is another of those quintessential English village occasions where the whole village turns out to have a good time and raise money for a good cause. In 2014, they were raising funds for the village hall. Not only did they have an extremely enjoyable day, they collected almost £2,000.

The fête is just one of Brayford's many fundraising initiatives across the year. Every August, there is a strawberry cream tea, to raise funds for the Methodist chapel, and a regular 'puddings and song' choral session in the church. The official photographer for the village, Madeleine Brownell, produces a calendar to raise money. She had sold out by Christmas, raising another £2,500 for the village, this time to fund cushions for the pews in the church.

I don't suppose Brayford is very different from many English villages in its cohesive enthusiasm for local initiatives. Geoff Dunford, chairman of the village hall trustees and one of the organisers of the duck race, reckons there is never a problem getting people to volunteer. He puts it down to the fact that a good proportion of those living in the village were born and bred there, went to the local school and never moved away, finding jobs locally, so they have retained a special attachment to the place – just like Johnny, really.

Hand's up if you want to play this game – Johnny at the Brayford duck race MADELEINE BROWNELL

And the winner is….. WENDY McLEAN

9. Birds of Summer

A nuthatch – a resident on Johnny and Julie's land
JOHNNY KINGDOM

'GET UP EARLY and listen to the birds, that will start your day right,' is one of Johnny Kingdom's favourite expressions. True to his own word, he's often out at dawn to hear the chorus of birdsong on his land.

Exmoor is a bird lover's paradise. You can see birds on the moor throughout the year and across all its different landscapes. It's the variety of landscape, in a relatively small geographical area, that makes Exmoor so bird-friendly. Like many other parts of the country the moor has in the last fifty years suffered from agricultural change: loss of hedgerows, increasing use of chemical insecticides and pesticides and a reduction in nesting sites for birds such as barn owls, though habitats congenial to birds have had more protection here than in other parts of the country.

The woodlands around Tarr Steps, Horner and Hawkcombe are National Nature Reserves. As well as being rich in lichens, fungi and broadleaved trees, they are home to a wide variety of woodland birds including treecreeper, nuthatch, spotted and green woodpecker and pied flycatcher, as well as varieties of tits. Sparrowhawks hunt them all.

On the coast you can see migratory waders and ducks, shelduck, cormorants, oystercatchers, curlews and egrets, especially in the middle of a freezing winter. Herons, dippers, sand martins and the odd kingfisher patrol the rivers, while summer on the high moor is alive with the sound of skylarks and home to stonechats.

Above them patrol birds of prey: buzzards and kestrels, even the odd merlin on the high moor and peregrine falcons on the cliffs. At night you might hear the different varieties of owl hunting: little owl, tawny and Johnny's favourite, the barn owl. He's been watching this cornucopia of bird life for as long as he can remember and filming it for as long as he's owned a camera.

Some of his most enchanting encounters with birds have taken place in locations as varied as his local church porch (swallows building a nest on top of that of a blue tit); the entrance to his cabin (clusters of wrens keeping warm in winter); the branch of a tree in his street (rescuing a pigeon chick); in a roll of sellotape in a mate's barn (a pied flycatcher's nest); in the room in which he edits (an injured buzzard); and even in the bottom of a hide from which he was filming, where a family of barn owls nested.

You would have had to have spent years out of the country not to know that barn owls are much

A barn owl JOHNNY KINGDOM

A little owl JOHNNY KINGDOM

A tawny owl JOHNNY KINGDOM

less common than they used to be. The intensification of farming and the gentrification of the countryside have hit them hard. There are fewer barns and old agricultural buildings, many having been converted into expensive homes, others demolished. As if that was not bad enough, we've managed to get rid of much of their preferred habitat. Barn owls love to hunt across rough grass; they are not especially fond of manicured fields and, these days, too much of the countryside is manicured. Luckily, parts of Exmoor still have the sort of rough terrain that is home to small rodents, shrews and mice, the food source that the barn owl enjoys.

However, not everything we've messed about with in the countryside is bad for barn owls. According to surveys conducted by The Barn Owl Trust, the majority of today's recorded nesting sites are boxes put up by people specifically for the purpose of attracting them. That's what Johnny has done on his land but, frustratingly for him, no barn owls have yet taken up residence. If they ever do, it's likely they will remain for years. Once a barn owl has occupied a good nesting site it will stay put, as long as it can be out of sight.

In the absence of owls close at hand, Johnny has always had to go out searching for them. It's not difficult to distinguish them from other varieties of owl. They have very large white heads and a white underbelly, with a wide wingspan. They are not keen on woodland, preferring open, rough country and they hunt from the air rather than from a roost. Johnny reckons the very best time to see them is twilight, one of their favourite times for hunting. You might hear them too, though if you hear hooting at night, that's not a barn owl but the cry of the tawny owl. The barn owl's distinctive call is a hiss or screech, not quite so romantic a sound.

Johnny has had many encounters with barn owls. While he was filming in the summer of 2014, he was tipped off about a nest box in a building not far from his home. He rigged a camera that

Bringing home supper
JOHNNY KINGDOM

was sensitive to movement so it faced the inside of the structure and was amazed to find that he had captured a male and female with no less than four chicks almost as big as their parents.

But perhaps his most memorable encounter with a family of barn owls came about in the summer of 2011, through pure serendipity, while he was filming a short series of television programmes about birds on Exmoor.

He was very keen to film barn owls for the series and, knowing that none had nested on his land, he spent days scouring the moor, searching high and low for a site, to no avail. Then, as summer was beginning to turn into autumn, he had a tremendous piece of luck in the last place he expected. He had built, but only rarely used, a hide on land owned by his friend Tony Thorne. He'd filmed excellent shots of a tawny owl in a nest box not far from the hide, but he had never seen a barn owl anywhere near there. Then, quite by chance, he saw an adult barn owl fly into the bottom of the hide itself.

With some technical help from Rupert, our cameraman, he rigged a couple of night vision cameras to watch the nest and then waited about a hundred yards away. The shots he eventually captured showed three barn owl chicks just days before they fledged, as well as wonderful pictures of the mother. In one remarkable sequence she called to the chicks, summoning them to perch on the edge of the nest, tempting them with a small mammal in her beak. But instead of feeding it to them she flew away, encouraging the young to take their first flight in her wake. Nervously at first, one by one, they followed their mum into the night sky.

This was barn owl behaviour he had never before witnessed, seen by the sheerest chance after days of searching the moor. Patience and persistence had paid off and you can imagine how pleased he was. But it's not the only time Johnny has filmed extraordinary bird behaviour that has been going on right under his nose.

A camera inside a small bird box close to the shack on his land gave him a thrilling insight into the night time behaviour of wrens. The winter of 2009/10 brought some bitterly cold nights and Johnny noticed that his camera in the box was recording a wren coming into the warmth of the nest. Then on the film he saw another, then another, and another. Eventually his camera captured no fewer than eighteen wrens cramming themselves into the box, huddling together for protection from the freezing temperatures.

Johnny should not have been quite as surprised as he was. The wren is Britain's most common breeding bird. Estimates put their numbers at more than eight million and their preferred habitat is woodland of the sort Johnny owns. The greatest threat to them is a bout of severe weather, which can decimate a population. So it is not that uncommon for them to spend the night tucked up in numbers for warmth. But to capture that on film is indeed unusual.

Filming a great spotted woodpecker's nest proved a more ambitious challenge. Johnny found its roost on his land after tracing the source of the drumming sound the bird makes. Some people imagine this distinctive tapping is the woodpecker drilling a hole for its nest. It is, in fact, the

Let's forget the gadget Bob –
Johnny managed this photograph of a
great spotted woodpecker on his own
JOHNNY KINGDOM

noise it makes to attract the opposite sex. Woodpeckers invariably nest in readymade holes in trees.

To try for the shot he wanted, Johnny sought the assistance and technical skills of his mate Bob Sampson. Bob had come up trumps in the past, inventing gadgets to help Johnny film badgers and they imagined they could do something similar with a pole, designed by Bob, to which Johnny would attach a small camera. Unfortunately, the pole was too flexible, the wind too strong and the woodpecker too canny. The best shot Johnny was able to get was from a hide near the tree in which the woodpecker had made its home. Not a perfect result this time but then again, as he often says, 'If you don't try, you never know.'

The wrens and the great spotted woodpecker are just two of the many varieties of birds Johnny has been able to film on his own land. He believes that if you treat birds well by putting out plenty of food and water, they will repay you handsomely. That's as true for someone with a small garden as it is in his woodland. In the winter, when there is not much other food about, there is often a goldfinch, a chaffinch, a few pied wagtails and even woodpeckers on his birdfeeders, while an ever-present robin sits on a branch and thrushes gorge on rowan berries in the wood. Down on the pond, there's a less welcome grey heron: 'He keeps eating all the fish,' grumbles Johnny. In spring he's had a Canada goose with no less than five goslings in the nest, which chuffed him no end.

When it's impossible to get close to a nest Johnny will often look for feeding sites. Wanting to film a small flock of spoonbills near the coast revealed the lengths he was prepared to go to in order to get his shot. It was impossible to build a hide on the mudflats because they were feeding on a tidal estuary. The solution he devised was imaginative, even for him. He decided the only way he could get close enough to the birds was in a hide that floated on the water.

Johnny duly designed a light timber frame on which he could mount a camouflage hide, building it outside his house and transporting it to the estuary on his truck. Having assembled it, he rigged two slings to fit over his shoulders to carry the heavy hide to the water's edge to float it towards the birds. It worked – to an extent. He was able to sit on the frame and film with a hand held camera without actually sinking. But though he did get reasonably close to the spoonbills, he discovered how much closer he could get to other waders feeding on the receding tide. He was especially taken by some shelduck and a flock of diminutive, and much more common, dunlin.

On other occasions, filming takes rather less effort, as was the case with a family of kestrels he spotted in the summer of 2014.

Kestrels are most often seen overhead as you drive along a main road. They hunt by using superb eyesight rather than smell or hearing. They hover 15 to 30 feet above the ground, facing the wind, their body and wings keeping them perfectly still, while they survey the ground for shrews, voles or other small mammals or lizards. Most people recognize them by their pointed wings, long tail and grey speckled underbelly. You will only rarely notice the reddish brown feathers of the body.

Not five minutes' drive from where Johnny lives, a local landowner told him about a pair of

A goldfinch in the wood
JOHNNY KINGDOM

If you cannot beat 'em, join 'em – the floating hide

A shelduck JON WHITE

A kestrel – note the colour and shape of the feathers
JOHNNY KINGDOM

Knowing me knowing you – Tommy getting stronger all the time JOHNNY KINGDOM

kestrels nesting on the concrete ledge of an old outbuilding. Johnny was able to watch and film the family at a safe distance before the chicks were, unfortunately, taken by jackdaws.

The kestrel is one of the more common birds of prey in Britain, though no longer the most common. Some estimates put the number of breeding pairs at 46,000 but numbers have fluctuated over the decades and have been dropping alarmingly again in recent years, due to the intensification of farming which makes their diet of small mammals more difficult to find.

Looking at Johnny's photograph of the kestrel, you can see the features that distinguish them as members of the falcon family.

Falcons typically have long, thin, tapered wings enabling them to fly at great speed and change direction in mid-flight. Their beaks are adapted to the way they hunt, with a notch that allows them to tear the flesh of a captured animal held in the claws.

Buzzards, on the other hand, are members of the hawk family. Hawks are generally bigger than falcons but slower, with a shorter wing span. Their beaks are smoother and they use their claws to kill prey. There are thought to be more than 50,000 breeding pairs in Britain and Exmoor has more than its fair share, where they soar on thermals over woodlands and open countryside, scanning it for prey. With a bulky body and short neck and tail they are easy to distinguish.

Johnny has filmed buzzards many times but perhaps his most remarkable encounter was in the

winter of 2006, when one fell into his lap. It was brought to him by a neighbour, Deana, who found it lying at the edge of a road, most likely a victim of a 'hit and run' accident with a car. With great presence of mind and a handy washing basket, she rescued it and took it to Johnny's house.

For more than two weeks Johnny became surrogate nurse to the injured bird. He took it to his local vet, who established that the buzzard, now called Tommy, had a badly damaged left wing. Nothing seemed broken and Johnny returned home with his patient. He kept it in a cage in his office so he could monitor its progress day and night. At first the bird would eat nothing and Johnny fretted that it would die. But it did not. Slowly, it recovered its strength and the breakthrough came when Johnny brought in some pheasant road kill. He cut off bits and offered them to the buzzard. To begin with Tommy snootily turned up his beak but gradually hunger got the better of him and he took pieces of flesh from Johnny's hand.

As the days went by Johnny watched Tommy exercise and strengthen his wings. Two and a half weeks later he considered his new best friend strong enough to return to the wild. On a wet and cold February morning Johnny and Deana, accompanied by the film crew, took Tommy to a piece of open land. They set up their cameras to film the bird as it shot through the open door of the cage, like an arrow leaving a bow. Tommy was once more free.

Free at last JOHNNY KINGDOM

10. Rivers

EXMOOR HAS beautiful rivers and some stunning riverside walks. There are fast-flowing rivers running north towards the Bristol Channel, while the Exe, the river from which Exmoor takes is name, flows south in a more gentle manner. But if there is one river that sums up all that is delightful about Exmoor for Johnny, it has to be the River Barle.

In high summer, on the stretch between Simonsbath and Dulverton, the Barle offers enticingly deep pools where swimmers can cool off. Trees shade long stretches of the riverside path and you will often find families picnicking. It's an ideal river for walkers in hot weather and, like all Exmoor's rivers, it's enjoyable at any time of the year.

Above: *Hoaroak Water – autumn*

Right: *A packhorse bridge across Horner Water*

Opposite: *The River Barle – summer*

Tarr Steps

However the enduring memory of the Barle for myself and Johnny is of winter rather than summer. New Year's Eve, 2011, was bitterly cold but at lunchtime the sun shone bright as a ball of fire. The sky was a deep blue and I had arranged to meet Johnny and Julie for a bite to eat at one of the most alluring spots on the Barle and indeed on the whole of Exmoor, Tarr Steps.

Tarr Steps is not so much a bridge as a causeway of flat stone slabs, spanning a series of stone piers. These structures are known as 'clapper bridges' and this is one of the largest of its type in Britain. Everyone has a view about how old they are. Some think they are prehistoric, others believe them to be medieval. In reality no one really knows. There was almost certainly a ford across the river at this point well before anyone laid stones over it.

I was on Exmoor to spend New Year at one of the most spectacular bed and breakfasts in the area, Cloutsham Farm. The man who was to become Controller of Factual Programmes at ITV was joining our party for the celebrations and we were beginning with a walk with Johnny and Julie, from Tarr Steps along the north bank of the Barle, followed by lunch in a pub just up the hill.

We met in the car park and headed along the valley. Johnny was in his element, identifying small birds flitting through the coppiced woodland as shafts of winter sunlight glistened on the

Tarr Steps – late autumn

running water. We saw a wren and had a conversation about whether the wren or the goldcrest is Britain's smallest bird; we never decided. We were out for about an hour before turning back, freezing cold but satisfied we had earned a fireside lunch in the warmth of the bar.

By the time we were back in the car park, more visitors were about. There were several 'Hello, Johnny' calls from walkers (there always are) then, as we were wishing each other happy New Year, a young woman came over and hugged him. Before we knew it she'd called the rest of her family, children, husband, father-in-law, dog and, in all probability, Uncle Tom Cobbley, to join in for a group photograph with him. No matter how persuasively Johnny tried to introduce his series producer and the very important man from ITV, the young woman had eyes only for the former gravedigger. She was in raptures about his last TV series, desperate to know when the next one would be and telling anyone who would listen how much the whole family loved his programmes. I think the commissioning editor must have thought we had paid her but then a crowd gathered, chipping in with more pleas for another series.

Finally we wished Johnny and Julie a Happy New Year and clambered into our car. The commissioning editor remained thoughtfully quiet for a while, then began to talk about what we had just witnessed. He reckoned he'd never seen a reception like it for any other TV presenter and could not remember anyone having quite such a popular appeal. He was overwhelmed and I sensed we had a strong chance of getting Johnny back on television before too long – thanks to Tarr Steps weaving its ancient enchantment.

The Barle has to be one of the most beautiful rivers in the country and, while it isn't possible to walk its length in full, it's worth visiting some of the places that hold a special meaning for Johnny.

In summer as good a place as any to begin is where the river rises, the high moor known as the Chains and its source at Pinkery Pond.

Pinkery Pond

Pinkery Pond seems as remote and timeless as the moorland that surrounds it. Compared with most ponds and bogs in the area of the Chains it's large and deep. There is a desolate, eerie feeling here, nothing about this landscape seems natural and it comes as no surprise to discover that the pond is man-made. The 7-acre site was dug in the 1820s by the man we've come across before, the Midland iron manufacturer, John Knight, who purchased Exmoor Royal Forest from the Crown in 1818. To be more accurate, the pond was created by the labours of about two hundred Irish navvies. But why? There are many theories, the most convincing coming from a man who strode Exmoor for years, producing a magnificent book on the history of the Royal Forest.

Roger A. Burton, author of *The Heritage of Exmoor* (Barnstaple 1989), argues that Pinkery Pond was part of John Knight's grand design to improve the quality of the soil. Burton believes that Knight had a plan to link Simonsbath to Porlock with a series of canals and locks, in order to

transport lime from South Wales. The lime would be landed at the small dock at Porlock Weir then brought over the hills by canal to sweeten the acidic peat moors. The purpose of the pond was to provide a reservoir for the canal which, like many of Knight's ambitious plans for the moor, was never completed.

Whatever its purpose, it's a wonderfully atmospheric place. The best approach is from the south, where the water is held back by a large retaining wall. The river flows, or trickles in summer, through a gully the men cut in the south-east corner of the pond. From there, it cascades into the valley below.

The Barle Valley is sternly beautiful, especially in places where tributaries have cut deep gullies that join the river above Simonsbath. The valley floor is flat-bottomed which makes the ground quite wet. The marsh grasses and rushes in these boggy areas are a wildlife heaven. The terrain is so spongy that it can be hard to plot a way through; bright green sphagnum moss is all there is between you and a soaking. These marshes are home to damp-loving plants: bog asphodel, common cotton grass, and heath spotted orchids.

There are marsh thistles and, feeding on them, butterfly varieties such as small copper, meadow brown and small tortoiseshell. On a late July afternoon, it can be serene.

Top: *Wild angelica spreads across the marsh on the upper Barle*

Above: *A small copper butterfly feeds on a thistle in the valley of the Barle*

Left: *The source of the most serene river on the moor, the Barle*

Opposite: *The eerie stillness of Pinkery Pond*

The river is on the right – the manmade waterway on the left

Top: The rack saw

Above: Tim Marriott and Graham Wills – volunteers at Simonsbath Saw Mill

Simonsbath

Sadly it's not possible to follow the river by footpath the whole 5 miles to Simonsbath, the village many people believe to be the 'capital' of Exmoor. Instead you have to use the road. As you reach Simonsbath the building on the right just before the bridge is a reminder the valley has an industrial past. It is a restored saw mill that was at one time powered by the river. A channel brought water from the moor above Ashcombe and later another more powerful leat was cut from the Barle itself to drive a water turbine. The mill was part of the Fortesque Estate and the machinery in it used for cutting and shaping wood for gates, posts and timber frames for estate properties. Today, the mill belongs to the National Park and is run by a small group of dedicated volunteers. It is open to the public on the third Monday of every month, all year round.

You can follow the public footpath behind it back to the weir, where water was taken off the river and into the leat.

This manmade watercourse runs straight for a little over half a mile and its water powered the turbine. The turbine in turn powered a series of belts that drove machinery, including a rack saw, in the mill itself. The mill had a forge that would have been used by a blacksmith making, amongst other handy implements, gate latches.

The place was designed so that lifting timber could be minimised. On the north side of the mill is an opening where logs could be stored to be simply rolled onto the feed for the circular saw.

The system worked well until the devastating floods of 1952 diverted the course of the Barle, rendering its water almost useless for powering the machinery. The estate called it a day and instead installed a diesel engine. These days water is used pretty much only for display and education.

Unusually for Exmoor there's a choice of places to get a cup of tea in Simonsbath. Boevey's, a tea room in a converted barn, is open from 10.30am to 5pm in the summer and until 4.30pm in the winter. It's named after James Boevey, who purchased a part of the Royal Forest in 1652 when Cromwell's government sold off a collection of royal properties and estates. He built and lived in the large house in Simonsbath, now in part a hotel. He soon acquired something of a reputation, annoying Exmoor farmers (never a good idea) by doubling the rates he charged for grazing stock in the Forest. Then, in 1675, he tried to claim the commons of all parishes bordering the Forest. If he had succeeded it would have meant that sheep farmers would have paid their tithes to him, rather than the Church. It's not difficult to imagine the reaction of both the Church and the farmers. They were probably grumbling about 'bloody incomers'. Boevey lost the case.

When but only when, the tea room is closed it's possible to get tea and cake from the house to which the barn was at one time attached, now the Simonsbath House Hotel. It's worth the effort (though tea and cake is always worth the effort) if only for the view of the river valley running east from the hotel. That alone is worth the extra money you'll need to fork out.

Not a bad place to enjoy a pot of tea – the Barle from the terrace at Simonsbath House Hotel

Sherdon Hutch

A few miles downriver from Simonsbath, the Barle is joined from the south by a tributary, Sherdon Water. This is one of Exmoor's most idyllic places, a favourite with Johnny for all sorts of reasons. It's a great location to watch and film wildlife, an ideal spot to picnic with the family and the place where he successfully encouraged one of his television commissioning editors to swim in the river.

Not many people pass by Sherdon Hutch – the public footpath seems to disappear – but the terrain here used to be traversed by one of Exmoor's most romantic figures, Hope Bourne. For many years Hope lived in a caravan some way up the valley of Sherdon Water, in a spot called Ferny Ball. Almost everyone on Exmoor knew Hope Bourne and Johnny was no exception. What they shared was a compelling, almost obsessive, love of Exmoor's wildlife and landscape. Johnny captured it on video while Hope captured it in her writing, articles, essays and books and her simple watercolour paintings.

She lived alone, without the comforts of modern life. She would walk from Ferny Ball to the small shop in Withypool for any basics she could not grow, collect or shoot. Hope cut a distinctive, if diminutive, figure striding across the moor with an old walking stick, her head covered in a shawl if it was raining. She had few friends but many acquaintances, Johnny included. Few people knew much about her past, though no one seemed to worry. Exmoor seemed to absorb her

as one of its own.

I met her in 1991 and, talking about Exmoor, she said this:

'Exmoor is a place where you feel the force of nature and the force of the weather. We are high and we get all that the Atlantic can throw at us. In the winter, we get hard weather from the north too and I've known it all. I've been lucky, I've not been snowed in for more than three weeks.

'The great thing about Exmoor is to preserve what is left of its wild character. The thing that matters here is what is left of the wilderness. It's something we need: we need our roots and our roots are not in civilisation.'

Hope was eventually persuaded to move from her remote caravan to the relative comfort of a small house in village of Withypool where she died in August 2010. Since her death there has been a deluge of books, videos, and interest in her life. One wonders what she would have made of it all. My hunch is that she would have been embarrassed by the publicity she is now getting, though I could be wrong.

Landacre Bridge

The Barle carries on past Sherdon Hutch and is crossed in its next stretch by Landacre Bridge, a beautiful five arch bridge that is said to date from the late medieval period – around the 1500s in old money. Its fabulous pointed arches are best seen from the west, especially in the afternoon sun, when the river and bridge are in perfect harmony.

Johnny enjoys it for another reason. In the past he has found it a good place to spot salmon making their way up the river in late autumn to their spawning grounds higher up the moor. It's hard to find them these days because there are so few but it was not always the case. When Johnny was a younger man salmon were prolific on Exmoor, coming up the rivers in the autumn to spawn in streams on the high moor. Then young salmon would make their way back to the sea, returning again after years to the stream in which they were born. On their route they provided sport for fly fishermen and meals for farmers and poachers, another of nature's miracles – the salmon that is, not the poachers.

Today there are far fewer salmon in Exmoor's rivers and no one seems to know with any certainty why. There are theories: one concerns the phenomenal growth of farmed salmon. These days you cannot move in a Scottish loch for huge pens full of farmed salmon and, because they are farmed in confined spaces, they are vulnerable to disease and sea lice. There is far too much organophosphate pumped into these salmon for their own good or the wild salmon's, or indeed ours.

Neither has the intensification of farming on the moors helped. The ideal environment for very young salmon are pools overhung with trees and shrubs, where they can feed on flies. Too many of these are disappearing as farmers 'clean' the river banks, allowing stock to graze the land right down to the river. As the habitat changes, the insects that are food for the growing salmon become less prolific.

Landacre Bridge at its best

Withypool

Little over two miles downstream from Landacre is the ancient village of Withypool with another delightful bridge, this one Victorian rather than medieval.

The best day to be in Withypool is the third Wednesday in August, the day of the Withypool Flower Show, which you will find up the hill in the village hall and the accompanying fete in a field beside the river. This is one of those lovely, old-fashioned occasions that remind you of a dandelion-and-burdock world with more bicycles than cars. The countryside is brimming with summer village fêtes and flower shows but still they come as a pleasant surprise to townies like me.

The roll call of past committee members reads like a chronicle of Exmoor dynasties: Bawden, Huxtable, Westcott, Scoins and Clatworthy among them. The event, which goes back to the early years of the last century, has seen some notable landmarks. In 1966 it hosted *Any Questions*; in 1972 it did not take place at all because poor weather meant there were not enough flowers in Withypool gardens to hold a competition; foot-and-mouth disease took its toll in 2001, the year the fête moved permanently down the hill to its present site beside the river.

These days there will be three to four hundred entries, ranging from fruit scones to onions, a considerable credit to the organisers, led by the redoubtable Secretary, Jill Scoins.

Down the hill at the fête fun and games for all ages carry on through the afternoon. There's an excellent second-hand book stall as well as the ever-present cake sale, with the cheapest cream teas to be found on Exmoor.

Jill reckons the flower show is Withypool's biggest day of the year because: 'It brings the whole village together.' The 2014 event raised a record amount of £1,600 for the village hall fund which, in these times of austerity, must mean they are doing quite a lot right.

But if you can't make Withypool on the third Wednesday in August, fear not. It's still possible to get a tea and splendid cake, or scones and cream, just over the bridge at the village tea room. It is run by Anita Howard who, as well as serving the food, makes it all. Her cakes are out of this world. I ordered one of her most popular offerings from the menu, coffee and walnut cake. I could see at once why it was so popular. I dare not go back, my waistline can't handle the experience.

Anita's coffee and walnut cake

The sponge cake ingredients are simple:

  4 eggs

  The same weight of self-raising flour, margarine and caster sugar

  2 to 3 teaspoons of coffee powder, dissolved in a few drops of water.

Heat the oven to 160C, gas mark 4. Beat the margarine and sugar, then add the eggs, flour and coffee and put the mixture into two tins. Bake it for 30 mins, then allow it to cool as you prepare the icing. For this, beat together 6 oz of margarine and 12 oz of icing sugar. Finish with a handful of walnut halves to decorate the cake.

From Top: *Jill Scoins with her prize winning 'Collection of Garden Flowers'*

Cream tea – Withypool

Anita Howard – cake maker and café owner – Withypool

Coffee and walnut cake and coffee –
Withypool

Across the road, the village shop is run by Anita's husband, Tony. It's like a Tardis, apparently small from the outside but it sells almost everything. Tony has been defeated only once since he started running the shop in November 1997. He failed to stock wax discs and labels for a holidaymaker cooking jam. Not a bad record I think. He's not unduly worried by the supermarkets he says because the older people in the village never stopped shopping here and now he finds younger locals coming back to supporting village shops, as Tesco has found to its cost and its plummeting share price.

Dane's Brook

About 8 miles downstream from Withypool lies another magical place on this magical river, the point at which the Barle meets another tributary coming from the south, Dane's Brook. There are a number ways to approach it. It's possible to walk upstream to it from Marsh Bridge near the town of Dulverton. An alternative is to drive up the southern ridge road. The road climbs from Marsh Bridge and at the top of the hill is Hinam Cross, with a right turning and a farm track to Hinam Farm. Park at the farm and walk down the steep lane to the river.

Is this the most idyllic place on
Exmoor? – Dane's Brook joins the
Barle

Whichever way one attempts it the confluence of Dane's Brook and the Barle is a spot not to be missed. It is just so beautiful. In spring the woodland floor is covered in bluebells and wild garlic, in early summer marsh marigolds find a home in the soft ground where the rivers meet and, in late summer, it's possible to wander along the riverbank and harvest blackberries.

If you sit long enough you will see dippers, grey heron and possibly, kingfishers darting along the river.

The location is drenched in history. Two of the most important Iron Age sites on Exmoor, Mounsey and Brewer's Castle, are nearby, though their dominant position overlooking the river is masked by the trees and saplings that cover the slopes. You'll find the remains of a packhorse bridge too, though recent storms have left it very much the worse for wear with one side missing and trees piled up against its concrete pillars,.

The walk along the river is sumptuous but so is the reception waiting for anyone who decides to reach Dane's Brook by parking at Hinam Farm. Esther Hancox opens her doors from Wednesday to Sunday for light lunches, teas, cakes and cream teas – and what cakes! She has a fantastic range. The café is open from the beginning of April to the end of October but Esther reassures me that if walkers turn up at other times, she will always manage a pot of tea or coffee.

Top: *A victim of the storms – a horse bridge across the Barle*

Above: *Esther and Colin Hancox take a break from farming and catering*

Left: *Hinam Farm in early autumn*

The location of the farm is another attraction, nestling in sheltered fields above the river. It is a favourite place for red deer and therefore for Johnny. The farmer Colin Hancox is an obliging sort and in the autumn he'll take Johnny out to where the deer are rutting, in one of the most spectacular settings on Exmoor.

Dulverton

From Dane's Brook, the Barle winds its way south through Dulverton (with more tea shops!) where you can picnic on the banks of the now wide and deep river at the town bridge. But before it leaves the National Park to join the River Exe at Exbridge, the river has one more story to tell.

Though no lives were lost on the Barle at the time of the Lynmouth floods of 1952, the water wreaked havoc in Dulverton. Images from towns devastated by floods, commonplace in Britain today, were rare and shocking then. In fact, so shocked was the British public in August 1952 that appeals went out and funds were raised to send help, including bananas, for the victims. The bananas were to be collected from Exmoor House. Today it's the HQ of the National Park Authority but in an earlier time it was the parish workhouse, so there was a certain irony that the relief was handed out from such a place.

The offices of the National Park – once the workhouse

11. The Moor in Summer

WHILE YOU CAN enjoy Exmoor's woodlands, coast and rivers at any time of the year, the place that really comes into its own in July and August is the high moor. Grass and heather moorland are without doubt the crowning glory of Exmoor's summer.

Broadly speaking there are two areas of high moor, with differing soil and vegetation and contrasting landscapes. One is the area of grass moorland known as the Chains, once the Royal Forest. The other is heather moorland. Heather moorland is disappearing in Britain and Europe at a rate that suggests it is going out of fashion but not on Exmoor.

Winsford Hill in August

The Chains – The Crown of Exmoor

If you want peace and quiet, stunning scenery and breathtaking views on a summer day, try walking up to the classic grass moor, the Chains. Even on a hot day when Lynmouth, not 10 miles away on the coast, is bursting with tourists, you can enjoy the high moor in virtual solitude. The Chains is the remote crown of Exmoor. A wonderful place to experience its atmosphere is close to one of the Bronze Age barrows that lie between the headwaters of the multitude of rivers running off the crown.

As you stand at an altitude of 1598 feet on Chains Barrow, with only skylarks for company, it's hard to imagine that thousands of years ago this area would have been much busier. The people who populated it would have had a much more serious purpose than your casual stroll. The round tumps on top of the hills are Bronze Age burial mounds, some dating back nearly four and half thousand years. In those times the lower slopes were thickly wooded and the barrows and standing stones would have been vital indicators of safe routes, a source of spring water, or maybe a sacred place of ritual.

This is at the heart of the area that was, from the eleventh to the nineteenth century, Exmoor's Royal Forest. It's quite different from other parts of the moor; it feels more remote and it is indeed more remote. It was seen as wasteland and reserved by the King for hunting. Over the centuries, Exmoor farmers bought rights to graze stock on the Royal Forest in exchange for rents, until it was sold to John Knight in the early years of the nineteenth Century. There is no woodland in this forest; it is a predominantly wet, grassy, boggy landscape with its own distinctive wildlife. Sheep graze here, though many fewer than in the days when farmers would turn their flocks onto the Forest and pay a fee for the privilege. There are few red deer and Exmoor ponies but what is missing in terms of animal numbers is made up for in unsurpassed views and the knowledge that, even in summer, you will have large swathes of it to yourself.

A combination of sphagnum moss and spongy but dangerously uneven, sedge grasses makes walking tough going. As you lunge across the uneven surface skylarks trilling as they spiral upwards are your only company. You have to watch your step but it is worth every ounce of effort since you have the sensation that here you are on top of the world.

At least that was my experience when on a hot summer's day in 2014 I walked to Chains Barrow from the Youth Hostel close to Goat Hill Bridge on the B3358 Simonsbath to Challacombe Road. After about forty-five minutes walking I crossed a stile, followed the well-marked path leading to the barrow and sat down on a bank to eat a picnic lunch. I was completely alone in the silence which was pure bliss. Then, out of the blue, I was joined by a skylark. At least I assumed it was a skylark. The solitary bird circled me, soared high into the air, then returned and perched on a fence post close to me and my lunch. It looked quizzically at me, an intruder on its territory. Then it soared once more, only to return again, this time holding an insect in its beak. I sat motionless and gazed in awe. I must have been closer to its nest than I realised so, after watching this wonder of the natural world for around a quarter of an hour, I finished my lunch and

Is it a skylark, a meadow pipit or maybe a spotted flycatcher?

The path leading to Chains Barrow

left the bird in peace.

It was only when I returned home and examined the photos I had taken that an element of doubt crept in. Was it a skylark? Or... had my companion actually been a meadow pipit?

You can decide for yourself. They're both small brown birds. I'm sticking with skylark – it has a more romantic ring.

Some people reckon that Chains Barrow is the perfect place on Exmoor, a spot where in every direction you can understand the topography of the landscape and why it is so special. Standing on the barrow itself, looking east some 14 miles, you can see Dunkery Beacon, at 1704 feet the highest point in Exmoor and Somerset. The rivers that flow from the northerly slopes of the Chains cut deep, steep-sided valleys. They carry fast flowing rivers, the East and West Lyn, Badgworthy Water, Hoaroak and Farley Waters which cascade through broad-leafed woodland on a short, rollercoaster journey towards Lynmouth and the coast.

Looking south through the heat haze you might glimpse Dartmoor. To the west it's easy to pick out Hartland Point on the North Devon coast. The landscape unfolding south of the Chains is more gentle and rolling and the two principal rivers of the moor, the Barle and the Exe, lack the drama of those flowing north. What they have instead is a lovely serenity. On the day I was walking, the valley of the Barle was lit brilliantly in late afternoon sun, the deep tributaries which cut into the principal channel showing perfectly in the low light.

It's an ethereal setting, yet what has shaped the natural history and its associated wildlife more than anything is something as mundane as the predominant soil type on the Chains: peat.

The Chains is a peat-covered dome. The accumulation of millions of years of rotting vegetation has left the area with an acid-rich, black earth, not much use to anyone trying to farm without tons

Below left: *Chains Barrow – towards Hartland Point*

Below right: *Chains Barrow – towards the Barle*

and tons of lime being poured on to it. However, people who lived here did find one invaluable use for it. Peat burns well and they cut it and used it on open fires, giving off a smouldering heat that kept out the chill in winter.

Not much of any value grew on the peat-based soil: just sedge grasses and sphagnum moss, rushes that poor people gathered and used instead of candles and summer flowering cotton grasses. But peat has a useful property. It holds water. It behaves like a giant sponge, retaining millions of gallons from some of the heaviest rainfall in England and releasing it slowly into the rivers that spill off it.

At least, that was until a dramatic and unpredicted rainstorm hit the area on the 15th and 16th of August 1952. The giant sponge could absorb only so much water and nine inches of rain poured onto an already sodden moor in twenty-four hours. It was as if a giant fist descended on the sponge, releasing a flood that descended on the coastal town of Lynmouth and resulting in 34 deaths and a hundred homes washed away.

However, too much water on the Chains was very much an exception. One of the problems the area has faced in recent years is too little water and the high moor has been slowly drying out. It's the result of excessive and effective drainage. Farmers and landowners have for years been cutting deep ditches and draining the moor so they could farm it. Old peat diggings, the legacy of people cutting it for fuel, did not help.

The consequence of the drying-out has been the gradual loss of a rare habitat. Bogs were disappearing and, with them, the plants and wildlife they supported.

Recently the authorities have been trying to reverse the process, bringing back water and reclaiming some endangered habitats. They have been helped enormously by the wet summers of recent years but the trick is to devise ways of holding water by blocking the drainage channels. If you visit some of the locations where they have been at work, you can see how they are doing it. They are using peat, wood and bales of straw to block some of the channels to make the grass moor wetter in the summer and restore some of the bogs. The initiative might have been called the Exmoor Bogs Project but for some reason they decided to call it the Exmoor Mires Project. One can imagine why.

Some of the restoration work is evident in the plants and flowers. In the summer months cotton grass blows gently in the breeze and as well as sphagnum moss, you can see sun dew, bog asphodel and common tormentil, with dragonflies and butterflies darting above the bogs – sorry, mires.

The heather moors

The heather moors are what most people recognise as the soul of Exmoor, spaces where you can see Exmoor ponies grazing, rare fritillary butterflies darting about, skylarks singing and red deer grazing. These areas are at their very best in August, a kaleidoscope of contrasting colours when bell heather and cross leaved heather combine in an intense pink and purple haze as the ling comes into flower.

North Hill, the coastal heath between Minehead and Porlock, the area around Dunkery Beacon

Top: *A peat bog, or these days, a mire*

Above: *Hare's tail cotton grass blows gently in the wind*

August on a heather moor

Opposite: *Heather swayling –*
North Hill SAM BRISTOW

A relative newcomer to the common –
Highland cattle

and the southern ridge, running west from Anstey and Winsford Hill are all distinctive but perhaps the best known is that stretching from the high point of Exmoor at Dunkery across to Porlock.

In the midst of these colours you can see herds of Exmoor ponies grazing the commons, red deer roaming the valleys and, earlier in the summer, the rare heath fritillary bouncing on the winds.

Many of these heather moors are protected through agreements struck between local farmers and agencies such as the National Trust, the National Park and Natural England, the government body that tries to balance the needs of agriculture and the environment. But that does not mean they are safe. They have to be managed every bit as much as the pasture that surrounds them. If the heathers that grow here are to retain their vibrancy, they need to be regularly rejuvenated.

You can see the evidence of this by looking at the differing shades of growth of heathers on the moor. Every year, in late winter, and certainly before ground nesting birds have begun to build, sections of heather are set alight in a controlled burn. It's called 'swayling'. The carbon left behind after the older, woody heather is burnt off rejuvenates the plants and the ground. Planned swayling means that different sections are burned in succeeding years and it is this that gives rise to the different shades and patterns in the landscape.

Landscape management doesn't stop at burning. Many of the animals you see on the commons are there to help keep the heather healthy and abundant. Ponies and sheep have been joined in

Top: *The team at the Periwinkle tea room – Vera Creech, waitress – Sue Rivers, cake maker – Hayley Richards, manager*

Above: *A choice of three jams with the cream tea – what's not to like?*

recent years by a newcomer, Highland cattle. There are small herds of this distinctive, wide-shouldered, large-horned breed on a number of commons. Richard Westcott, a tenant of the National Trust at Wilmersham Farm close to Stoke Pero, receives grants to keep a small herd of Highland cattle on Wilmersham Common. He reckons Natural England and the Trust like the cattle because they are heavy on the ground and break up unwanted vegetation, though it can be a surprise when you first come across them. As for the meat that Richard has had from them, he says it is beautiful and very tender, though there is not as much of it as from more traditional Devon or English breeds.

But even the enormous jaws and appetite of Highland cattle cannot do much about one of the more serious problems that threatens to harm the heather moorland: bracken.

In the summer, its green fronds contrast brilliantly with the purple heather and, as it turns a golden brown in September, bracken marks the passing of the season. The difficulty is that there is too much of it. It's similar to the rhododendron problem along the coast. Allowed to grow unchecked, bracken invades the heather moors and will eventually wipe out the very plants that make them distinctive.

It's another legacy of modern farming. In times past farmers cut bracken and used it as bedding for stock. Cutting it two or three times a year kept it in check but these days farmers don't need it so don't cut it. Animals don't eat it so for once they cannot help in landscape management. It's an ongoing problem, one that needs a solution urgently if we are to keep the rare quality of these landscapes which define Exmoor.

If you have been walking through the bracken or heather on North Hill, one of the areas of open moorland especially attractive in the summer, it's worth heading for one of Exmoor's most picturesque villages nearby, Selworthy, and one of its most delightful tea gardens. Who knows, you might even have a flash of inspiration over a cup of tea and the wonderful array of cakes and scones and come up with a solution to a tricky land management problem, or how to spot a red deer when the world and his wife is out with a video camera.

The cakes are all made by Sue Rivers, baker at the Periwinkle, a café close to Selworthy church, where you can park. You can't miss it; the church is painted white and stands out in the landscape more clearly than the beacon on top of the hill. There are fabulous views from the church and car park to enjoy before you dive into one of Sue's offerings.

Tragically the Periwinkle is open only until the end of October. But Vera and the café manager, Hayley, will make sure that after enjoying the heather you will enjoy your cream tea with a choice of jams, including whortleberry. I don't know if the berries are picked nearby, but they work well with the abundance of thick clotted cream and leaf tea in real china cups. The scones with the cream tea absolutely melt in the mouth but one of her specialities is lemon meringue. It's a tough choice. You'll just have to go back again so you can try both.

PART FOUR
AUTUMN

12. It's the Taking Part that Counts
Johnny's Autumn

Julie Christian and Ceri Keene – who made it all possible

Exford vexillologist – Robin Ashburner

Previous page: *Autumn on Dunkery Hill*

IT WAS A COLD, blustery morning in late October at Minehead railway station. The crowd waited with bated breath for the arrival of a special steam hauled train. For enthusiasts, the engine was one of the West Somerset Railway's fleet of steam locomotives, a 1925 built Somerset and Dorset Joint Railway SDJR 7F 2-8-0, number 88.

The wind cut through the warmest of clothes but the air was laced with anticipation. The train, due at 11.46 am, was carrying Johnny and Julie and a very special package: the winning entry in a competition to design a flag for Exmoor. Among the throng of onlookers on the platform were the five finalists.

The event, organised by Ceri Keene and Julie Christian, from Brushford near Dulverton, was a major part of the celebrations marking the 60th anniversary of the National Park. The women had

run a public awareness campaign and 261 designs had been submitted by people of all ages.

The organisers were lucky to have on hand to help them Robin Ashburner, one of Britain's foremost vexillologists (flag expert) and a leading flag designer and maker. A past President of the Flag Institute, Robin lives and works in Exford where he designs and cuts the patterns for all the flags made by his company. Though he is a Welsh farmer by instinct and history, Robin has been involved in flag design since 1969 when he worked on the investiture of the Prince of Wales in Caernarfon.

In August, a panel that included Johnny, Robin, Ceri and Julie reduced the 261 entries to just five, which were then put before the public in a secret vote.

The judges found it hard to choose but the public had less of a problem. One design, submitted by Jenny Stevens,

The Somerset and Dorset Joint Railway 7F
STEVE EDGE – www.wsr.org.uk

And the winner is – Jenny Stevens

Julie, Johnny, Jenny and Ceri celebrate

attracted a whopping 41% of the 858 votes cast. Let no one say that the democratic imperative on Exmoor is er, flagging.

Jenny's design, in her own words, 'tells the story of Exmoor's varied terrain – sea meets river, meets cliff path, meets moorland, meets wildlife.' It included the head of a stag, almost compulsory on anything to do with Exmoor and was emblazoned on the tank of the 7F as it pulled into Minehead station.

After the speeches, the photographs and the paparazzi (was it an otherwise quiet news day that morning in Minehead?), flags were presented to the mayors of five local towns. Then Johnny and Julie his wife set off on a bus to present flags to representatives of some of Exmoor's villages. It was going to be a long day.

And it was a day that, for Johnny, coincided with his busiest time of year. Autumn on his land means dozens of nest boxes to clean out, they must be emptied of old nests and eggs that failed to hatch in the summer and be made ready for birds to nest the following spring. Some of the boxes are designed with a metal plate on the front to prevent predators pecking away the wood making the hole big enough to seize chicks inside.

Johnny emptying his nest boxes

A grey heron emptying his pond
JOHNNY KINGDOM

Away from his land he's busy with safaris. Since the days of his first badger hide people have wanted to go out onto the moor with him and autumn remains the most popular time of the year, because it includes the spectacle of the red deer rut.

The day before a safari Johnny will recce locations where there might be deer. As long as they are not disturbed there's a fair chance the stags and hinds will remain there overnight. Then he works out an itinerary so that he is ready to meet the visitors early in the morning, always the best time to see deer. Then he will be off, through woodland, over moor, sharing his insider knowledge with the clients. It's a great way to see and learn about parts of Exmoor you might not otherwise reach.

When Johnny first offered safaris there were only two or three others doing the same. These days there are at least nine companies driving visitors around, all chasing the same wildlife and the same clients. 'It's much harder than it used to be,' Johnny says.

A safari can be organised by emailing him at safaris@johnnykingdom.co.uk. Book early to avoid disappointment, as they say!

Autumn is also busy with engagements he just cannot miss, like the annual red deer 'bolving'

Best not give up your day job –
Johnny bolving JASON BALL

competition. It's one of those festive rites that have become part of the warp and weft of Exmoor. It would be nice to think the tradition goes back to the mists of time but in fact it is very much a twenty-first century invention. Well, all traditions were 'new' once upon a time!

It began, like many traditional activities, in a pub, in this case the Rock Inn at Dulverton. Two locals, Phil Ferris and Elvis Afanasenco, were having a friendly argument about who could sound more like a roaring stag. To resolve it they left the pub and had a go. Let's be honest there's not that much to do in Dulverton of an evening.

They enjoyed it so much they decided do it every year, inviting their friends to take part. The first formal competition was won by Phil and when he died in December 2004 his mates decided to honour his memory by competing annually for a shield in his name. Proceeds from the evening go to the Devon Air Ambulance. Phil's sister Chrissie is one of the fundraisers and her skills in fundraising would leave even Bob Geldof speechless. Chrissie sits in the doorway to the pub making sure no one gets in without contributing to the fund.

The actual competition takes place high above the River Barle at Draydon Rails. It is open to anyone who thinks they can make a sound like the roar of a stag. The event always draws a crowd of curious onlookers as well as willing (and sometimes unwilling) 'bolvers'. Johnny has entered the contest in the past and did so in 2014 but it is safe to assume that he is better at filming deer than sounding like them. The winner that year was Rob Follett who, coincidentally, happened to be the person who carved the Phil Ferris shield.

For anyone who wants to seek out this most Exmoor of Exmoor traditions, it takes place on a Saturday evening towards the end of October: check with the Rock Inn or the Exmoor National Park website for specific dates and times. Or you could just venture to Draydon Rails in the dark and have a go but I take no responsibility for what happens next. There is no evidence that anyone sounding too much like a stag has ever been pursued by one but you never know.

Phil Ferris – the man who started the bolving competition
CHRISSIE THOMAS

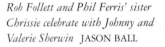

Rob Follett and Phil Ferris' sister Chrissie celebrate with Johnny and Valerie Sherwin JASON BALL

13. The Other Jewel in Exmoor's Crown – Exmoor Ponies

A winter coat keeps out the worst of the Exmoor winter
JOHNNY KINGDOM

Opposite: *Some of the herd on Winsford Hill*

WHEN PEOPLE VISIT Exmoor hoping to see red deer they're often disappointed. But if they come to see ponies they will almost always leave happy. And if they come in the autumn and witness one of the 'gatherings' they might leave exceedingly happy. It's a curious paradox, although there are greater numbers of deer on Exmoor, ponies are much more visible. They like to graze on the open commons and they don't run away when they catch sight of a passerby.

According to Sue McGeever, secretary of the Exmoor Pony Society, the organisation set up by farmers in 1921 to conserve this rare breed, there are about five hundred of the ponies on Exmoor. The herds are a mix of breeding mares, foals and a few stallions, one or two to each group of mares, living in concentrated areas on the commons.

The Rare Breeds Survival Trust has designated the Exmoor pony as 'endangered'. After World War Two Exmoor's ponies were seriously down in numbers. According to records there were as few as fifty, probably a result of too many ending up on the dinner tables of hungry locals while meat was rationed. Since then their fortunes have recovered and today there are more than 4,000 registered worldwide. In spite of this apparent success the Exmoor pony remains on the endangered list. The reason is the ponies' limited amount of genetic material: no amount of breeding can increase the genetic pool from the fifty founding ponies.

Many believe that the Exmoor pony is a direct descendant of the wild ponies that came to Britain more than 100,000 years ago. When a little later, human beings arrived, they at first hunted and then tamed the ponies as domestic animals. The first written mention of them in Britain is in the Domesday Book.

But to refer to today's Exmoor pony as a 'wild' animal is something of a misnomer. Though they live out on the commons all year round and are hardy enough to survive on the grazing available, they are the property of different farmers or landowners. The herds that run on Haddon Hill, North Hill and The Warren for example are owned by the National Park Authority. The owners decide which ponies will live, which will die, which will be kept on the commons to propagate the herd and which will be sold. Exmoor ponies have been managed and bred by farmers

in this way for centuries, with varying degrees of dedication and enthusiasm.

In the past they were kept as working animals. Before mechanisation ponies were the engine room of the farm, used for everything from carting and carrying to pulling ploughs. But twentieth century technology spelled the end of the line for the Exmoor pony as a working beast and their fortunes slumped in the 1930s and '40s threatening the extinction of the breed.

But in the 1960s, as numbers began to grow again, it was realised that the ponies performed two crucial roles on the moor. The first was public relations. The Exmoor pony is as much a symbol of Exmoor as the red deer. To lose the herds would harm tourism and the economy of the area.

Then, alongside their economic value, people also began to recognise their value as a tool of conservation. Sue Baker, an authority on Exmoor ponies, has spent years in the less than romantic study of their faeces and her research has shown that the grazing habits of the pony contribute uniquely to the quality of the heather on the commons, (one would hope for some revealing finding after putting oneself through the demands of such a study). Unlike sheep and cattle ponies over-winter on the commons. Evidence from their poo reveals that their diet changes with the passing of the seasons. As grasses become more scarce in the autumn the ponies feed on rushes, shoots and even gorse. This capacity to adapt has enlisted them as conservation volunteers and without them ever realising it.

A foal enjoying the summer grasses
JOHNNY KINGDOM

Because Exmoor ponies are considered useful for both the economy and the ecology of the moor, a tremendous amount of effort is now expended to keep the herd pure and the gene stock healthy. That was not always the case.

For many years ponies were crossbred with other breeds to 'improve' the stock, or they mated with other horses released on the moor by owners who could no longer afford to keep them. There was a danger that the purity of the breed would be lost. Exmoor's herds might easily have ended up like those on Dartmoor, with ponies being sold off the moor for as little as £1, or shot. Now the Exmoor Pony Society works with enlightened owners to ensure this does not happen.

One of them is the Milton family, friends of Johnny for many years. They own the herd on Withypool and West Anstey Commons which is known, not especially romantically, as 'Herd 23'. The Miltons have been farming on Exmoor since the early years of the nineteenth century and keeping ponies since 1818, when Nicholas Milton established the herd not long after the sale of the Royal Forest. Rex Milton took over from his great uncle Fred in the 1990s.

The day Johnny went to talk to his friend on West Anstey Common for one of our programmes Rex mused about his reasons for preserving the breed:

'It's part of our heritage. The Exmoor pony is part of Exmoor and if we don't bother with it, we'll lose that heritage.'

How lucrative are the ponies for farmers like Rex Johnny wondered? 'There's not great money to be made in the trade,' he reckoned. 'Some get sold for show, or for children to ride, but that's about it.' That's why he controls the numbers in his herd and believes breeding too many is irresponsible.

'What's the point of producing foals that no one wants? There are too many horses about as it is.'

Rex has sixteen mares on West Anstey with one stallion and nineteen mares and two stallions on Withypool Hill. 'I keep two stallions on Withypool because one is getting on and I want a younger one to take over gradually. If I put two mature males together, well, there will be no end of trouble.'

Mares used to come into season in the spring but in recent years it has tended to be earlier. Sue McGeever thinks this has to do with global warming: 'Everything seems earlier these days.' Foals are born after a gestation period which lasts on average 330 to 345 days, so ideally they would arrive the following spring when new grasses are just coming through and there is plenty to eat.

Summer is spent gorging on nutritious grasses, resting and posing for the many visitors who come with cameras. But the busy time is autumn when the 'gatherings' take place. A gathering is a roundup of all the ponies that belong to one owner. Rex Milton gathers his herd on Withypool Common on a Sunday in October and Johnny is usually there to watch and film the proceedings.

What happens is part of the intricate management of the quality of the herd and regulation of the numbers of ponies on the moor. The herd is driven across the common and into a natural funnel, where it is penned. That's the easy bit; the rest is somewhat trickier.

*Rex Milton driving some of Herd 23 to
the funnel – the start of a long day*

The ponies have to be counted by Rex and members of the Society. They want to know how many ponies are running on the common and whether any have died, or gone missing, during the year. In the gathering in the autumn of 2014, Rex's Herd 23 produced 20 foals out of 35 mares which is about par for the course in the tough conditions of Exmoor. The ponies' welfare will be checked and if any of the mares are looking ill or have problems they will be taken off the common. Sue McGeever waves her Darth Vader wand across their shoulders to read the microchip embedded there. Microchipping the ponies has been a practice since 2009. Nowadays not all are branded so Sue's microchip reader is sometimes the only method of identifying an individual pony.

It's surprising how much science is being employed in what is quintessentially a rustic scene. Pulling a few hairs out of each foal's tail is another part of the procedure. The society uses DNA data from the hair to match the foal with a mare and stallion, establishing its parentage.

Rex, his sons James and Tim and family friends separate the foals from their mothers, a process that requires both strength and fearlessness. The ponies can deliver a nasty kick and shin protectors come in handy. Once rounded up the foals are taken to the Milton's farm and kept overnight, ready for inspection by the Society the following morning. They are looking for the characteristics which define the 'true' Exmoor pony.

The first thing the Society considers is the foal's general appearance, shape and colour. Seen out on the moor Exmoor ponies are instantly recognisable: stocky, round-ribbed and barrel-chested, with a broad back and a distinctive coat that has a bright sheen, its colour varying from light to deep reddish brown. In the autumn they grow an extra weatherproof layer, like a thick overcoat, with more hair and a greasy look and feel that provides natural insulation throughout winter. The underbelly is lighter in colour.

Separating foals from their mothers – leg guards essential

Exmoor ponies have a distinctive 'mealy' coloured muzzle and a 'toad eye' which means they have large, wide-apart prominent eyes with pads of fat above and below. A pony must not have white hair anywhere; the inspectors check for white on the hooves and soles, in the tail and mane and on the body. The tail itself is vital to the wellbeing of the pony, a sort of drainpipe which allows rain (and there is plenty of it where the ponies live) to run off its back efficiently.

An Exmoor has an immensely strong jaw and set of teeth; it needs them because munching through tough gorse and grasses in winter is not for the faint-hearted. The jawline must be straight, with the front incisors meeting cleanly. Ears should be short, thick and pointed.

All foals born out of registered parents are themselves registered and their details entered in the stud book, in Section One for those that meet the breed standard and Section X for those that do not. But every foal gets a second chance and can be re-inspected.

At this point their owners will decide how many, if any, of the foals will rejoin their mothers back on the common. Some fillies and one or two colts might go back, depending on whether the landowner wants to increase, or merely maintain, stock levels.

A classic Exmoor in a classic setting

Foals that don't go back on the commons, or those that fail inspection, are put up for sale as riding ponies. How much is an Exmoor pony worth? Rex Milton reckons a registered Exmoor can fetch between £300 and £400 but for one that fails, the price is much lower, maybe £100.

The Miltons' autumn gathering turned out well. Of the twenty foals Rex brought in, 18 were registered into Section One, two into Section X. Two fillies went back out onto Withypool Common and one colt to West Anstey.

For owners who don't get the balance right, producing foals they cannot sell, the Moorland Mousie Trust can come to the rescue. The Trust is a small charity set up in 2000 by Valerie Sherwin, a woman passionate about the interests and welfare of the Exmoor pony. The Trust runs the Exmoor Pony Centre which has rescued more than five hundred unwanted ponies. Most are fostered out for conservation grazing in other parts of the country but there is a resident population of around twenty mares and foals at the centre.

Fortunately, Rex Milton did not need the Trust's help. By Christmas 2014, eleven of his remaining foals had been sold for showing and riding, some as far away as Germany,. His daughter, Rosie, used social media to sell five of them, an online trend that Rex admits leaves him bemused. I'm with him there.

14. Sheep

RED DEER AND Exmoor ponies might be amongst the area's most popular tourist attractions but there's something very reassuring about a field of sheep munching grass in the late afternoon sun. You will find plenty of that on Exmoor. But to assume they are merely a pretty pastoral sight is to underestimate the part sheep play in making the moor look the way it does today.

Sheep have been the mainstay of the Exmoor economy for thousands of years. Apart from low-lying Porlock Vale most of Exmoor is too high, too wet, and too cold to support arable farming so from time out of mind farmers have relied on sheep, supplemented by beef cattle, to make a living from the land.

The mainstay of the Exmoor economy for thousands of years

And just as Exmoor is alive with sheep, it's full of sheep farmers. You can see them at the markets, wizened men for the most part, with flat caps and ruddy faces. Many wear a tie and tweeds; there's not much denim amongst this tribe. You will see them watching and listening intently as an auctioneer sings out the market prices for fat lambs, rams, or whatever is up for sale.

There are dozens of sheep farmers on the moor but two that Johnny has known for many years are, in their different ways, typical of the breed.

David Bawden represents the sixth generation of his family to run sheep at Cloggs Farm. With around 375 acres of land and help from his wife and son, his aunt Gwen and a couple of sheep dogs, he looks after five hundred breeding ewes. Perched above the steep valley of the outstandingly beautiful Dane's Brook the farm is high, more than 1000 feet above sea level.

Kathy Stevens became a tenant at Cloutsham Farm which is owned by the National Trust in 1987 and from 1990 single-handedly (with some help at busy times) ran a flock of 500 breeding ewes even while she was building up a hugely successful bed and breakfast enterprise. Then in 2000 David Greenwood arrived and they have been partners ever since.

The farmhouses themselves hold a number of clues about the way sheep have shaped the look of Exmoor. Cloggs Farm is an outstanding example of a Devon long house and its setting is

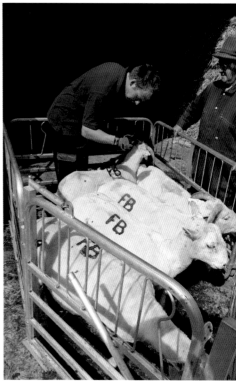

Andrew Bawden and his great aunt Gwen still mark their sheep in the name of his grandfather Fred Bawden
MELANIE DAVIES

Left: *Kathy Stevens and David Greenwood outside Cloutsham Farm*

Opposite: *David Bawden feeding his flock of Exmoor Horns*

Cloggs Farm

Cloutsham Farm

especially striking. It stands alone in the middle of the surrounding farmland, at some distance from any other settlement or village.

The same is true of Cloutsham Farm, also at 1000 feet above sea level. In the seventeenth century it comprised two shepherd's cottages and was extended by its then owners, the Acland family, in 1886. They added the Swiss-style veranda you will see today and used it as a hunting lodge. Admiring its incredibly beautiful location from across the valley on Dunkery Hill, what stands out again is its isolation.

This sense of isolation at Cloutsham and Cloggs is no accident. The farms are typical of dwellings in hill, sheep farming landscapes and very different from arable farming country.

In the days before modern technology arable farmers needed a plethora of skills close at hand and the farms and the men who had those skills tended to be huddled together in villages where you would find, as well as farm labourers, blacksmiths, wheelwrights and saddlers to service the horse driven economy. Over the centuries the social institution of the village developed and then thrived in those parts of England where arable farming predominated.

Sheep farming was totally different. It did not require the number of hands or ancillary activities demanded by arable farming. There were no large numbers of men needed to mind teams of horses or oxen for ploughing or to keep farm equipment in good shape or to bring in the harvest. Sheep farmers had little use of a blacksmith or wheelwright. Lambing and shearing were the only occasions when a farmer might need to call on help, for the rest of the year he (and it invariably used to be a he) could cope alone, with a wife, a son, or a shepherd and a good dog.

What was important was that he was close to his sheep, to check they were in good shape during lambing or to turn them the right way up if they became stuck on their backs. Because a sheep farmer needed to be able to get around his farm quickly, the farmhouse tended to be in the middle of the holding.

Sheep on Brendon Common

Sheep farmers needed not villages but markets, places where they could buy and sell stock, meet others or simply exchange views about the weather or prices. I bumped into both David Bawden and Kathy Stevens at a local market while researching this book. Neither was buying or selling but they were there all the same.

So this was one way sheep husbandry shaped the way Exmoor looks today: a landscape of isolated farms and flourishing markets but few villages.

Grazing too played a part. Sheep need lots of land and if the quality of the grass is poor, as some of it is on Exmoor, they need yet more of it. Over the centuries sheep farmers relied on much more than the grass in their own fields to feed their flocks. One source of grazing was the Royal Forest and, from Saxon times until the Forest was sold in 1818, farmers paid to graze sheep there. It's been estimated that in the later years of the fourteenth century up to 40,000 sheep were driven up and onto the Forest during the summer months.

The commons played a role also. Farmers had access to commons and sheep would spend time on them before being brought back to the shelter of the fields close to the farm for the winter. Sheep grazing gave Exmoor's commons a particular look. Apart from grass, sheep ate young shoots, and their perpetual summer munching prevented woodland from developing, leaving space for the distinctive heathers to flourish.

Striking a balance was crucial. Too many sheep and the commons would be overgrazed and look like bald heads; too few and there was a risk the land would turn to scrub and trees take over. So the number of sheep on the moor was critical, determined in part by prices at market and in part by the quality of grazing on the acidic peat soils. The grass was always poor and a limiting factor on the numbers of sheep farmers could keep. The lime kilns along the coast suggest that farmers tried constantly to improve the sweetness of the grazing and the productivity of the soil.

During the 1930s the development of artificial fertilisers and feed supplements helped improve productivity so that more sheep could graze on every acre of ground. But the price lamb fetched at market also played a crucial role in regulating numbers. In the years between the two World Wars sheep farming, like all farming in Britain, went through a slump. Prices fell and farmers found it hard to compete with lamb imported from the Empire. As the number of sheep on the moor dropped their effectiveness in keeping down scrub diminished and the quality of the heather moor declined.

Top: *Exmoor Horns at Cloggs*

Above: *David Bawden's prize winning Exmoor mule shearlings*
MELANIE DAVIES

The fortunes of sheep farmers and the moor itself changed considerably after World War Two. The 1945 Labour Government recognised that, without hill farmers, the uplands would 'go back' and be of little use to anyone so a decision was taken to pay hill farmers a subsidy to encourage them to continue to farm there. The payments, based on the number of breeding ewes on the farm, were known as 'headage' payments. These, along with guaranteed subsidised prices for meat, encouraged hill farmers to expand flocks.

Encouraged to keep as many sheep as possible Exmoor farmers turned some of the traditional moorland into green fields. With new techniques of hay and silage making and new dietary supplements sheep numbers grew. However by the late 1950s many people thought the pendulum had swung too far and that the commons were now in danger of being over-grazed or even lost all together, destroying the very character of the Exmoor landscape that sheep were supposed to sustain. These days the impact of sheep on the environment and landscape is acknowledged in different government schemes to support hill farmers.

Guaranteed prices have long gone and headage payments were scrapped in 1993. Since then successive governments have introduced various incentives to encourage farmers to graze fewer sheep on the commons, focusing instead on restoring the quality of the landscape. David Bawden, at Cloggs and Kathy Stevens and David Greenwood at Cloutsham, have struck agreements to keep fewer sheep on the moor through a series of compensatory environmental payments. These are, in effect, inducements to restrict stock levels and restore the landscape to something like it was in the past. As the creeping numbers of silver birch bushes on Dunkery Beacon's lower slopes suggest, getting the balance right is a dark art rather than an exact science.

Alongside sheep numbers, sheep husbandry has played a role in shaping the character of the moor. Over the centuries farmers selectively bred sheep that they found most suited the sort of terrain they farmed so types of sheep began to acquire names that linked to a particular place. The Swaledale came from a particular valley in the Yorkshire Dales, the Devon Close Wool from that county and the Scottish Black Face from north of the border. The variety most closely associated with Exmoor was the Exmoor Horn, a hardy animal that could withstand rough weather and wet winters and could give birth without much help from the farmer.

This is the breed on Cloggs Farm, and David Bawden, a past President of the Exmoor Horn Breeders Association, has a breeding strategy carefully planned to sustain the Exmoor Horn on his farm. To maintain a healthy number for the future he uses his Exmoor Horn rams to cover 150 pure bred Exmoor Horn ewes. The rams can cost quite a bit: David paid 700 guineas for one in 2014 at a sale at Cutcombe Market.

At the same time he crosses another 250 Exmoor Horn ewes with Blueface Leicester rams, to produce 160 Exmoor 'mule' shearlings. (A 'mule' is the offspring resulting from the mating of any upland ewe with a Blueface Leicester ram.) The picture shows a pen of twenty of them. They won second prize and achieved the highest price at the Exmoor Horn annual breeding sale which takes place every September at Blackmoor Gate Market. He sells the lambs in the autumn, for either immediate slaughter (fat lambs) or for 'finishing' on lower ground (store lambs).

There are fortnightly sales of sheep at Blackmoor Gate. The anticipation of farmers there, wanting to know how prices are moving, is palpable. One of them is David Greenwood, Kathy Stevens's partner, who brings old ewes as well as store lambs across the moor from Cloutsham to sell at the market. He reckons the prices are better there than at Cutcombe, the market closer to his farm.

But the sheep David Greenwood sells are not Exmoor Horns. They are a different breed and come from a different farming tradition on the moor.

Most of the 500 breeding ewes at Cloutsham Farm are Cheviots. Kathy has kept them for as long as she has been there; she prefers them to the Exmoor Horn and reckons butchers like the longer lamb that the Cheviot produces.

As the name suggests they are not native to Exmoor. The breed comes from the north of England and the Scottish Borders. The ones at Cloutsham and at a dozen or so other farms spread mainly across the western stretches of Exmoor, are a legacy of the family which stamped its personality on the moor in the nineteenth century. John Knight bought most of the Royal Forest from the Crown in 1818, intending to enclose it and plough the land. But when that failed he did

Prices being called at Blackmoor Gate market

A Cheviot ewe at Cloutsham waits anxiously for November 6th

what other landowners in the area had been doing for generations, grazed his holding with sheep.

However, he broke with the local tradition of rearing Exmoor Horns. His view was that the breed was not robust enough to survive the harsh winters on the high moor so he introduced Cheviots and some Scottish Blackface sheep which he believed to be hardier breeds. It was tough going. Knight made the mistake of trying to farm his 16,000 acre estate with only his three sons and a few hired hands. Left to fend on the high moor during the winter months, the Cheviot turned out to be just as problematic as the Exmoor Horn.

John's son, Frederic took over the estate in 1841 and he, like his father, turned to the Cheviot. Father and son must have harboured some obstinate and deep-seated grudge against Exmoor Horns, refusing to take advice from all the other sheep farmers in the area. However, unlike his father, Frederic decided that the best way to farm the sheep was to not to go it alone but to farm with the help of shepherds who had experience of the breed.

Unfortunately, shepherds who understood Cheviots lived in the far north but Frederic had the audacity to persuade a number of them to travel with their flocks from Scotland to Exmoor and rent farms he built for them. Considering the state of transport in the 1860s this was a truly remarkable enterprise. Some of the shepherds who took up his invitation travelled to Bristol by train and then drove their flocks to Exmoor on foot. The descendants of some of these shepherds continue to live on the moor but their legacy in terms of the breed they brought with them is to be found on farms like Cloutsham.

Sheep define the rhythm of the year on these upland farms. Putting rams and ewes together, 'tupping', is held back until late autumn. At Cloutsham in 2014, Kathy and David kept rams and ewes apart until November 5th. Then the fireworks really began, so to speak, across the whole of the sheep farming country on the high moor.

Delaying tupping in this way means lambs on the high moor are born late, in April, when it is warmer and grass is already growing. They graze through the summer and are sold in the autumn for slaughter or to 'finish' on lower ground. The weeks before Christmas are when the livestock markets come into their own. Ewes not sold in the autumn are brought down from the commons for the winter and the cycle begins once more, rolling on year after year, helping to keep Exmoor the distinctive landscape it remains today.

The Christmas market – Cutcombe

Is it my turn next? – November on Exmoor

14. Autumn on the Moor

'AUTUMN IS A second spring, when every leaf is a flower'. So said the writer and philosopher Albert Camus. Indeed, that is exactly how autumn feels on Exmoor. The range of broadleafed deciduous trees – oak, ash, beech, rowan, sweet chestnut, even rare whitebeams found nowhere else – tumbling down the coastal slopes or hugging river valleys, turning from shades of green to golden brown, ochre, vermilion, rust and other autumn colours, all at slightly different times, makes the season an unforgettable, as well as a majestic one for wildlife enthusiasts.

One of Johnny's favourite places on the moor in autumn is the huge expanse of woodland that lies between Dunkery Hill and Porlock. It is owned by the National Trust and is part of one of the largest bequests given to them, the Holnicote Estate. Its 12,000 acres contain some of the most valuable and unspoilt landscape in Britain and the estate has a remarkable history.

As you walk through its woodlands, over its heaths or through its ridiculously picturesque villages, it's difficult to believe that you are benefiting from the generosity of radical socialism. The whole of the estate was given to the nation in 1946 by its politically committed owner, Sir Richard Acland.

The Acland family had acquired the estate at Holnicote by marriage in the mid-eighteenth century. Though very much part of landed aristocracy and the political elite of their day successive Acland Baronets had, by the nineteenth century, moved politically leftwards, from the Peelite wing of the Tory Party to the Liberal Party. Sir Richard clearly had the family genes, at least the political ones. He had been Liberal MP for Barnstaple in the 1930s but he left the party in 1942 and, with J. B. Priestley amongst others, founded a socialist party called Common Wealth.

Sir Richard was opposed to inherited wealth, so bequeathing the estate to the National Trust and thereby to the nation must have seemed like the natural and decent thing to do. It is worth remembering that as you wander through the woodlands.

With an abundance of shelter, cover and food in the woods, the habitat is perfect for red deer. It is here you will see the biggest herds on the whole of the moor – and some of the biggest herds of deer watchers. Autumn is especially popular because considerable numbers, including Johnny, come to witness the annual rut.

And it's not just deer. Parts of the Holnicote Estate are considered so important that they have been given the status of National Nature Reserve. It's easy to understand why the area is so popular

Horner Woods – early autumn

Top: *Dormouse heroes –
Brian and Sheila Coulson*

Above: *That's about the size of it –
a semi torpid dormouse*
BRIAN COULSON

Right: *Wildlife heroes – Noel Allen
and Caroline Giddens*
EXMOOR NATURAL HISTORY
SOCIETY ARCHIVE

with wildlife enthusiasts: there is so much to choose from. A mix of dry and wet heath, together with deciduous woodland, makes for an invaluable habitat for bats; the estate has 15 out of the 17 varieties in Britain. The rare heath fritillary is one of many varieties of butterfly found here and more than three hundred varieties of lichen can be found in the woods.

Brian and Sheila Coulson's particular favourite is the dormouse. A mixed broadleaved woodland with hazel and plenty of ground cover provides one of Britain's smallest mammals with all the ingredients for their ideal diet: honeysuckle and pollen in the spring, fruit, nuts and beech mast in the summer and autumn. The lack of food in winter does not bother them, they hibernate. The dormouse is an endangered and protected species. In many parts of the country its habitat is shrinking so these managed woodlands, in which hazel is coppiced and groundcover plants such as brambles allowed to flourish, are especially important to its survival.

Dormice live most of their waking lives in the tree canopy and come down to ground level only to sleep off the winter in a nest under a tree or bush. They breed in the late summer; the Coulsons put out nest boxes on tree trunks for the female to use when she gives birth. Opening the nesting box puts incredible stress on the dormouse so Brian and Sheila restrict their research work to twice a year, once in the summer and once in October.

First, they secure the back of the box to prevent the occupant from nipping out through the rear door, then they gently remove the dormouse, put it in a plastic bag, weigh and sex it and check for any diseases or problems. The couple have been doing this since 2003 and Sheila says they learn more about the dormouse each year, including how not to get bitten by one; this diminutive creature packs a nasty nip.

It is highly specialised work and illegal unless, like Brian and Sheila, you possess a dormouse handling license. You might ask why they do it; the answer is sheer love. Their love of Exmoor in general and the dormouse in particular is channeled through a remarkable voluntary group, the Exmoor Natural History Society, founded in 1974 by a remarkable natural history enthusiast, Noel Allen.

Actually, to call Noel an 'enthusiast' seriously underplays his expertise and field craft. I first met him in 1990 when in the course of making a series of television programmes about the Exmoor landscape, I was the beneficiary of his patience, kindness, encyclopaedic knowledge and a seemingly unlimited supply of chocolate orange biscuits. What Noel didn't know about Exmoor's wildlife was not worth knowing.

He died in 2009 but the society he created, following a series of adult education lectures, continues in the tradition he established. It began in 1974 with just thirty members. When, in 2014, the society celebrated its 40th anniversary, membership had grown to more than 450. But if you fancy joining they could always do with more. The aims, 'to study and record the botanical and wildlife of Exmoor and to assist, where possible and desirable, in its preservation', have changed little over the years. But then neither has the secretary, Caroline Giddens. She became one of the founding members when she accepted an invitation from Noel to take on the role of the society's botanical recorder and she's recording still. At the end of the first year she and her volunteers had noted 604 species; today the number stands at 1,428. One could be forgiven for thinking that, after four decades, the volunteers have found all there is to find but every year new additions to the list reveal the work is never ending.

I joined a group of about ten, led by Sian Parry, on an autumn fungus foraging walk through the woods below Hawkcombe. The variety of woodland fungi is one of the reasons why the area is considered so special and autumn is the only time to see the huge range under foot.

Now let's be honest, many people are suspicious of fungi. They don't behave like 'normal' plants, it's hard to see where they come from and, because we don't understand them, we tend to be cautious. Since many grow in woodland, and our natural tendency is to be nervous in woods, it's not surprising that fungi are still regarded as devilry. Then again, the fact that some are highly poisonous and could actually kill you does little to promote their image.

In fact, as Sian explained on the forage, fungi are amazingly useful and essential to habitats, especially in woodland where they function as organic waste disposers. They do it by breaking down dead plant material into its chemical parts, thereby providing nutrients for plants and trees. A fungus will often have a symbiotic relationship with a tree, helping the tree take up water and vital salts and receiving sugar from its host in return.

Their role is vital to the rejuvenation of woodland and that is why the woodland managers on the Holnicote Estate actively encourage fungi. Walking through these woods you'll see rotting branches, tree stumps and healthy trees with a range of fungi growing on them. However, how to know what you are looking at is tricky, Sian is not always available and without someone like her it's handy to have a good fungi or mushroom guide book with you. Though it's not a good idea to pick them for eating unless you know what you are doing.

After exploring the estate, it's worth visiting the village of Horner. Tucked away there is a delightful tea garden which I used to avoid, mainly because I found it rarely open and, when it

Top: *Reversed clover – a recent discovery of the Exmoor Natural History Society* JEANNE WEBB

Above: *Birch Mazegill in Horner Woods*

was, it sold only cream teas. Now no one is more fond of a cream tea than myself but even I think there are limits. A cream tea is most definitely an afternoon experience, if your search for wildlife in the woods begins at dawn and you want a break at 11am a cream tea is perhaps not the most enticing item on the menu.

But to my delight the tea garden and the menu changed in 2014. It was taken over by a dynamic local, Laura Webber (Laura has to be local with a surname like Webber) and her approach is very different. She is keen to open the tearoom as often as possible and certainly every weekend, throughout the year. There is a woodburning stove and no longer is a cream tea the only choice – though I have to confess that, since I was there in the afternoon, I couldn't resist one.

As leaves in the Exmoor woods turn golden down in Porlock they harvest the fruits of the season or, to be more precise, the fruits of their community orchard. Late October sees a celebration of that most English of fruit, the apple. They make a big thing of Apple Day in Porlock: not only does the village grow its own apples but, tucked away in a small paddock behind the Visitor Centre, it has its own traditional wooden hand-cranked Somerset cider press.

It would be nice to think that the press had been there for years but it is a recent arrival, brought here in 2010 from a farm near Langport on the Somerset Levels, a more cider-focused part of the county and reassembled by Derek Purvis, the man behind the initiative. This beautiful oak specimen was built in 1862 when the product of the press was almost a currency, farmhands would be paid in part in cider. Making cider on the farm was a tradition that persisted until the 1960s,

Laura Webber – keeping Horner tea garden and me going

Opposite: *ENHS fungi expert Sian Parry*

Above: *Derek Purvis*

Left: *Building the cheese at Porlock Apple Day*

139

Lyn Purvis and Cathy Murtagh making fantastic use of apples at the Apple Day

Opposite: *Volunteers at Combe Orchard, Porlock take a welcome break*
BOB LOONEY

until technology and better opportunities in towns decimated the number of farmworkers and cider presses were left to rot, picturesque reminders of a vanished past. This one had a lucky escape, Derek brought it to Porlock and reassembled it.

On Apple Day people bring their apples and give them to Derek and a team of volunteers who wash and crush them. The apples are spread across the base of the press to build a 'cheese'. In times past straw was used to hold the crushed apples in place but these days hessian does the job. When the cheese is stacked a couple of volunteers with strong arms and strong backs crank the press and the golden juice pours out into a stone trough.

Laurie Lee called it 'golden fire' and, when you look at the colour as it comes out of the press, you can understand exactly what the great Gloucestershire writer meant.

Not to be outdone by their menfolk, Lyn Purvis, Derek's wife, and Cathy Murtagh produce a range of cakes and biscuits all made using apples. I was drawn especially to an unusual apple sauce cake made by Cathy which has been adapted from a traditional Somerset recipe.

Cathy's Apple Sauce Cake
Ingredients:
113g (4oz) butter
227g (8oz) soft brown sugar
1 large egg
1 large or 2 medium Bramley apples
227g (8oz) self-raising flour
1/2 teaspoon ground cloves
1/2 teaspoon ground nutmeg
1/2 teaspoon ground cinnamon
1/2 teaspoon salt or Lo-salt
113g (4oz) raisins
For the butter icing:
113g (4oz) butter
227g (8oz) icing sugar
A few drops vanilla essence

Pre-heat the oven to 180 degC / 350 degF / Gas mark 4, and grease and line a 20cm (8 inch) cake tin.

Make the apple sauce by peeling and chopping the apples, then bring them to the boil in a saucepan with a drop of water until they have become a pulp (no extra sugar needed). Set aside and allow to cool. In a bowl, combine the butter and sugar to a fluffy creamy texture. Add the beaten egg. Stir in the cool apple sauce, then the sifted flour, salt and spices and finally the raisins. Mix

well until everything is evenly distributed. Pour into the tin and bake in the oven for about an hour. Check near the end of baking time by inserting skewer into the cake. If it comes out clean, the cake is done, but if not put it back into the oven for another few minutes. Cool for five or ten minutes in the tin, then turn it out onto a wire rack.

To make the icing, combine the icing sugar, butter and vanilla essence in a bowl until smooth. Apply to the cake with a spatula or a shallow spoon.

Then eat it with warm cider – delicious!

The cider press is not the only apple-focused initiative in Porlock. For as long as anyone can remember Combe Orchard, belonging to the Porlock Manor Estate, had been in a poor state. The trees were old and untended, the ground beneath completely overgrown.

It stayed in that condition until the spring of 2009 when a group of residents negotiated with the estate and the tenant farmer who leased the land with a view to taking on the job of clearing and improving the orchard. They began with bare hands, spades and forks and cleared the ground. Then they started on the trees. Helped by small grants from bodies like the National Park they found an expert to identify those in the orchard. They discovered they had English varieties with lovely names: 'Reverend Wilkes', 'Blenheim Orange' and 'Lanes Prince Albert'. They learned how to prune those that could be saved and they planted new ones to replace those that couldn't. As well as thirty fruit trees they planted more than three hundred others to build an edible and biodiverse hedge and they put a fence around the whole thing to keep out hungry deer.

Today, volunteers spend a couple of days a month keeping the orchard in a sound state. In a good year they produce up to 600 bottles of pasteurised apple juice. The money they raise helps fund further developments in the orchard, like buying a shed where they can store tools. They have their own pasteurising unit and, for a nominal charge, they will press other people's apples too.

The people of Porlock are doing their bit to hold onto and preserve a past that would otherwise quietly disappear, to our greater loss. Bob Looney, one of the volunteers, reckons it's important to maintain the orchard in a traditional way, not only to keep traditional skills alive but to encourage biodiversity and bring back insects, small mammals and wild flowers.

The volunteers are doing on a small scale what some are doing on a larger canvas; taking crops from the land but working with nature rather than against it, to recreate a world that once was common but which we are in danger of losing altogether.

This is the landscape that Johnny Kingdom loves and celebrates in his films, an environment where every plant, every tree, every creature has its place, existing in a delicate balance where the smallest change wrought by us humans can have far-reaching effects. It's the place where Johnny has his roots, the place that shaped him, the place that has enabled him to share his love of nature with so many others.

Long may it continue.

Fruits of the forest

Postscript

IN EARLY JANUARY 2015, while I was in the final stages of writing this book, my father died. He had been admitted to hospital on Boxing Day 2014 with severe bronchitis and his ninety-three-year-old lungs just could not cope.

He wanted to come home to die, so my brother and I, with a lot of support from our families, cared for him in his last days. Not wanting to just sit beside his bed asking if he needed anything, I found myself reading to him draft chapters of the manuscript. He knew my work with Johnny and, in 2013, had spent an entertaining day with him on his land and later in the Corn Dolly tea shop in South Molton, so he knew something of Exmoor. My father had been a engineering worker all his life but after his retirement he and my mother joined a walking club in their home town. Walking liberated them. Most weekends and sometimes for whole weeks during the spring and summer months, off they would go in a mini bus with friends to walk a different part of our remarkable country. One time, in summer 1991, they went to Exmoor. They stayed at the Miltons' Partridge Arms Farm and spent a week out on the moor. I remember him telling me about one memorable walk from the top of Dunkery to Selworthy Beacon, not bad for a 70 year old. I hope he had a cream tea in the Periwinkle Café.

Joining that walking club was something of a rediscovery for my parents. My childhood memories include walks and picnics in the countryside we could reach from Crewe by bike, we didn't have a car. Those halcyon days would often involve picking wild fruit: bilberries, as we used to call whortleberries, damsons, or apples, which would end up that evening in a mouth-watering pie cooked by my mother. Looking back, I realise that those days must have been responsible for the way I came to love and appreciate the countryside.

Sitting beside his bed, reading aloud about red deer, barn owls or house-building for badgers I would sometimes get an thumbs-up or occasionally a shake of his head (he found speaking difficult under the oxygen mask under which his face was trapped), indicating his like or dislike of the writing. I'm delighted to say I received more approvals than disapprovals but I will always be sad that he was not able to hold this book in his hands and read the completed work.

David Parker
Bristol
February 2015

My dad – Howard Parker